Additional Praise for *Engaged Ownership*

Engaged Ownership is a succinct, fascinating and well-written treatment of a complex subject. Amelia brings a unique vision to the work; she comes from a fifth-generation family business and was a trust lawyer and family advisor before running her own family's business for over a dozen years. She now works with families on governance issues and is very much engaged in the process which is the subject of the book.

Joseph A. Field, Of Counsel, Withers Bergman LLP

Amelia has written the essential Owner's Manual for the family enterprise. This book is an indispensable resource for family business owners, operators, and shareholders, as well as those who work with them.

Jonathan H.F. Crystal, Executive Vice President, Crystal & Company

Amelia draws upon her personal and professional experiences to demystify the complicated and oft-misunderstood realm of family business. Engaged Ownership is a must-read for family business owners and financial professionals who work with these families.

Kurt Miscinski, President, HPM Partners

Engaged Ownership

Engaged Ownership

A GUIDE FOR OWNERS OF FAMILY BUSINESSES

Amelia Renkert-Thomas

WILEY

Published by John Wiley & Sons, Inc., Hoboken, New Jersey.
Published simultaneously in Canada.

For general information on our other products and services or for technical support, please contact our Customer Care Department within the United States at (800) 762-2974, outside the United States at (317) 572-3993 or fax (317) 572-4002.

Wiley publishes in a variety of print and electronic formats and by print-on-demand. Some material included with standard print versions of this book may not be included in e-books or in print-on-demand. If this book refers to media such as a CD or DVD that is not included in the version you purchased, you may download this material at http://booksupport.wiley.com. For more information about Wiley products, visit www.wiley.com.

Library of Congress Cataloging-in-Publication Data:
Names: Renkert-Thomas, Amelia, 1962-
Title: Engaged ownership : a guide for owners of family businesses /
    Amelia Renkert-Thomas ; foreword by Kenneth McCracken.
Description: Hoboken : Wiley, 2015. | Includes index.
Identifiers: LCCN 2015036765 (print) | LCCN 2015041896 (ebook) |
    ISBN 9781119171133 (hardback) | ISBN 9781119171171 (ePDF) |
    ISBN 9781119171157 (ePub) | ISBN 9781119171171 (pdf) | ISBN 9781119171157 (epub)
Subjects: LCSH: Family-owned business enterprises. | Small business—Management. |
    BISAC: BUSINESS & ECONOMICS / Small Business.
Classification: LCC HD62.25 .R46 2015 (print) | LCC HD62.25 (ebook) |
    DDC 658.02/2—dc23
LC record available at http://lccn.loc.gov/2015036765

Cover Design: Wiley
Cover Image: © 751/iStockphoto

Printed in the United States of America

10 9 8 7 6 5 4 3 2 1

To Jacob, Harry, Herman, J. Steven, Rachel, Ken, and Guy—entrepreneurs, teachers, partners.

And with deepest love and thanks to JSR for teaching me that if you don't like the game, change the playing field.

Contents

Foreword

The genesis of this book was Amelia's characteristically practical way of expressing the question that every enterprising family needs to answer at some point: What do the owners value about their enterprise?

Note that this question is not the same as *How* do the owners value their enterprise? When the question is framed that way discussion tends to focus on just the financial value and provokes a debate about which valuation method should be used. However, as every enterprising family and those who work with them know, a financial valuation provides only a partial answer to the question. So that is not good enough.

This is because one of the distinguishing features of family enterprises is that the owners attribute value to nonfinancial objectives. What they struggle with is how to identify, discuss, and enumerate these types of capital so that they can agree how to value them.

This book gives owners of a family enterprise a new way of dealing with these issues. It is based on what Amelia and I have learned from working together with family enterprises in different parts of the world over many years, but it is also of personal interest to Amelia as one of the owners of a fifth-generation family business. Using this extensive professional and personal experience, Amelia has been able to describe the different types of capital that a family could have invested in their enterprise, and for this she has coined the immensely useful term, *core capital*.

One of the refreshing aspects of this work is the way it highlights the important role of owners. Often ignored and even maligned as a problem in family enterprises, it is in fact their responsibility to become engaged and to enumerate the core capital of the enterprise. They also need to establish the forums and policies that will bring this all to life, which might include a new balance of power between owners and management that is very different from other types of business.

The concepts of engaged ownership and core capital will make immense good sense to family enterprises and their advisors. Unfortunately, it is unlikely to make as much sense to those who think that family businesses should all become more like public companies. In those companies, owners provide financial capital and power is concentrated in the hands of management. Short-term shareholder value remains the paramount goal no matter how much effort is made to fit in other types of return. This simply serves to illustrate that the reality of ownership in a family enterprise is fundamentally different from the public company model.

The importance of core capital and engaged ownership is ever present, but both will naturally come to the fore at critical junctures in the life of a family enterprise, such as during succession.

For example, when the original entrepreneur or wealth creator is passing on the product of their life's work, the notion of core capital will help the family to value the overall meaning of this inheritance. In later generations, the owners' ability to become engaged owners who can discuss and evaluate their core capital in a calm and rational manner will be vital to the continued success of the family and their enterprise. Even slight, unresolved differences of opinion among relatives could cause the type of rancorous conflict that destroys everything that a family has invested in their enterprise, meaning their relationships and reputations as much as their money.

These realities highlight the importance of understanding inherited ownership. Passing on ownership matters more in family businesses than other types of business because, to use Amelia's term, the inheritance represents the core capital that the family has already invested in their business as well as their hopes for the future.

It is important, as Amelia has done, to look at the effect of different types of ownership and not treat owners of a family enterprise as a homogeneous group. For example, how does a family ensure that a trust that holds shares will be aligned with their overall understanding of core capital and that the trustees will be effective as engaged owners?

Changing perspective, external investors in a family enterprise should seek to understand the core capital of the family owners and the ways in which they operate as engaged owners rather than make the error of trying to fit the family enterprise into another model of business, whether that be the public company or any other type.

This book is a significant and timely contribution to family enterprise knowledge and practice. It is an enjoyable read that will benefit families and advisors who are able to embrace new ideas in pursuit of improving their understanding of the fascinating and complex world of family enterprises.

Ken McCracken
International Family Business Consultant
United Kingdom
August 5, 2015

Preface

This book came about because I kept hearing a half-truth about family business succession presented as a best practice. More than one family business consultant opined that it is a bad idea for control to pass to owners who aren't "in the business." Lawyers recommended estate planning strategies that concentrated control in the hands of those managing the business, not only for tax mitigation but also to "reduce the risk of conflict." Bankers and wealth advisors laughed that "all business-owning families are dysfunctional."

Certainly, no family business—or family, for that matter—is without conflict. Conflict is endemic when people with different perspectives—owners, directors, managers, family—have different needs, perspectives, and priorities. And issues of control can be some of the most vexing problems family businesses can face.

But to suggest that consolidating control of a family business in the hands of management is a good way to avoid conflict—worse yet, a "best practice"—sells owners short. In our consulting practice I have met and worked with too many multigenerational owner groups where owners play a productive, active, and accepted role in business decision making to believe the half-truth so many advisors are perpetrating.

The challenge is: How can owners become engaged in business decision making in a way that sustains and builds the capital that has been created?

Owners who don't work in the business can be an asset, not a liability. They bring a different, but critical, viewpoint. They often possess skills, talents, experience, and perspective that can help shape the vision and strategic direction of the business. They, of all participants in the family business system, are best situated to think beyond "What's the best decision for the business?" to "What's the best decision for our family and our core capital?" Core capital—the unique blend of financial, human, and enterprise capital that make up the assets of a business-owning family—includes the business itself but goes far beyond it, and includes the savvy in the family's lineage and the entrepreneurial knowledge and drive developed over generations. For a business-owning family, there is so much more at stake than money. When owners think broadly about how all the forms of the family's capital are invested inside and outside the business—not just the financial capital—they are more likely to deploy their capital wisely.

This book is written for family business owners and the advisors who help them. It lays out a time-tested process for building engagement among all owners, managing and non-managing. My business partner and close colleague, Ken McCracken, and I, and the consultants who work with us, have used this process with families across the world over many years. We have found that engaged owners experience less conflict and bring important contributions to the business and the core capital. They have spent time together articulating a shared purpose—the answer to the question, "Why do we want to be owners of this business together, if at all?"—and laying out a common vision for the future. They have worked with board, management, and family to allocate responsibility for making decisions around critical issues such as capital investment, acquisitions and divestitures, dividends, strategic planning, corporate branding, and relocation, and have laid out policies to provide additional guidance. For family owners who undertake the work of engagement, there is a new energy around business and capital discussions. With engaged owners at the helm, board and management alike find they have a strategic partner and a far clearer vision for the future.

The process and challenges of achieving engaged ownership are illustrated throughout the book by the story of the Owen family, second- and third-generation owners of Owen Products, Ltd., a terracotta manufacturing company. The four Owen children—Mike, Martha, Amanda, and Christopher—find themselves as third-generation owners following the unexpected death of their father, Charlie. The Owens are entirely fictitious, but their story is pieced together from those of many family businesses, and it demonstrates how managing and non-managing owners can come together to make decisions about the future of the business and core capital.

Engaged Ownership contains four parts.

Part I: Engaged Ownership: An Introduction

Part I introduces the concept of *engaged ownership*—a different paradigm for family business owners. Engaged owners bring a deep understanding of their core capital and a vision for the future.

Chapter 1: More at Stake than Money

Chapter 1 introduces the concept of engaged ownership for family business. Family owners are regularly presented as the villains in media presentations of family businesses, but they can be a core strength of the business. Achieving engaged ownership requires owners and advisors alike to think differently about the roles and responsibilities of family owners, their shared purpose, and their collective vision for the future. To see owners in this new light, the discussion around business succession planning needs to change from *Who's going to run the company?* to *What is the best use of the core capital?* Core capital consists of financial capital, human capital, and enterprise capital. Chapter 1 also introduces three ownership constellations that make engaged ownership more difficult to achieve: the managing owner, the trust, and the non-family investor.

Chapter 2: Achieving Engaged Ownership

Chapter 2 provides an overview of how owners achieve engaged ownership. Owners must organize and lead the work to achieve engagement—it is not a process that the board or management can orchestrate. Owners will want to undertake the work of developing engagement when circumstances have changed and the natural governance system—"the way we do things around here"—no longer keeps the business in a comfortable equilibrium. This chapter discusses when owners should undertake the process of engagement and emphasizes the importance of undertaking engagement in connection with a significant transition. This chapter provides an overview of the engagement process: enumerating core capital and articulating shared purpose and vision.

Chapter 3: Engaged Ownership: Hallmarks and Impediments

Chapter 3 discusses the four hallmarks of engaged ownership: interest, understanding, ability, and longsightedness/broadsightedness. Engaged owners look beyond dividends to ask: What is our core capital? What is our shared purpose: Why do we choose to be owners of this business and its core capital together? What is our vision? This chapter also considers some of the impediments to engaged ownership: public company governance, conventional wisdom favoring controlling owners, focusing succession narrowly on the business rather than core capital, and denigration of inherited ownership.

Part II: Getting Organized

Part II provides a foundation for family business owners seeking to increase engagement.

Chapter 4: Family Business Roles and Relationships

Chapter 4 discusses four distinct roles in family businesses: owners, board, management/employees, and family. Each participant will occupy at least one role; some may occupy more than one or even all four. Each role has a distinct perspective:

- *Owners*—Owners hold the ultimate power to determine whether to keep, sell, expand, or contract the business. They may delegate decision-making power to other roles.
- *Board*—The board's primary role is as the chief overseer of the enterprise. The owners typically delegate to the board the responsibility for setting/approving strategy for the enterprise, hiring senior management, and monitoring performance.
- *Management and employees*—Management and employees operate the business in accordance with the strategic plan approved by the board.
- *Family*—The family is the source of the entrepreneurial spirit and values that lie at the core of business culture.

Each group will have its own focus and views about how the core capital should be deployed.

Chapter 5: The Legacy of the Past: Natural Governance, Family History, and Culture

Chapter 5 discusses how the decision-making system of a family business has evolved over its history.

Many family businesses from their first days evolve a form of natural governance that is largely based on assumptions, expectations, and understandings, rather than the tangible structures and policies of a formal decision-making system. This natural governance system might be called "how we do things around here." Natural governance is particularly apparent when a family business is run by a controlling owner. Natural governance can be adaptable and resilient, but as complexity increases, more formal decision-making processes may be necessary.

The business may come to be seen as a favored family member. However, engaged owners must have an ongoing conversation with board and family about how the core capital is being deployed, what risks and opportunities exist, and whether core capital should be redeployed in other ways, even if that might mean downsizing the existing business or exiting it altogether. A hallmark of engaged ownership is the ability to have difficult conversations about the future of the core capital, and, when necessary, to challenge long-held attitudes and assumptions.

Chapter 6: Enumerating Core Capital

Chapter 6 explains core capital: financial capital, human capital, and enterprise capital.

Profitability and positive cash flow will need to be achieved and sustained if the core capital in all its forms is to be sustained. A failing business will slowly destroy other forms of core capital as it consumes financial capital, while a successful business will sustain and grow financial and other forms of core capital.

Human capital is the total of the family's and the business's individual and collective human potential. Human capital includes social capital: relationships and connections; influence and values; goodwill and reputation.

Enterprise capital is all the unique knowhow embodied within the business and family; it is the array of one-of-a-kind combinations of capital that generate a return greater than what the separate elements would generate individually. Enterprise capital is the end result of human capital that has been coupled with financial capital to accomplish a specific endeavor.

Enumerating core capital is the exercise of thinking about all that has been invested in the business and the family over time—all the assets, in all forms, that make up their legacy and their future opportunity set.

Chapter 7: Shared Purpose

Chapter 7 describes how a group of owners can articulate their shared purpose. Shared purpose is the answer to the question: Why do we want to be owners of this business together, if at all?

For some owners, there is indeed an undeniable shared purpose and sense of collective focus and effort. For others, shared purpose can be more difficult to articulate, or even nonexistent. When there is a lack of shared purpose, it can be impossible to generate the energy and focus necessary to sustain engagement, particularly when an owner cannot reach consensus with other owners. Owners who feel bound together against their will run the risk of damaging the business. In such circumstances, facing up to the reality of the situation with honesty can help clarify the path forward.

Every owner will have a different perspective; the point is to see common threads and then work to articulate them clearly. A facilitator with family business experience can help to guide the work and keep discussion on track. Shared purpose can reunite and reenergize siblings and cousins who otherwise might not have reason to come together, and can foster a new sense of collaboration and consensus.

Chapter 8: Vision and Mission

Chapter 8 discusses how engaged owners articulate their vision for the future of the business and the core capital, and how they determine their mission for the coming two to five years.

Vision is the owners' collective vision of the future of the core capital and the business. It is the answer to the question: Now that we can articulate our shared purpose, what is our destination? What future do we see?

A clear and well-articulated vision animates the shared purpose: the owners can see the future and focus their efforts on achieving it. And while the shared purpose belongs to the owners as a group, the vision becomes the vision for the entire business and the core capital. It becomes the animating driver of the business. The owners' vision frames the board's discussion of strategy. It creates the direction and boundaries for management's deployment of resources. It gives family members an understanding of the purpose and direction of the business.

The goal of the mission exercise is to develop a list of steps that need to be undertaken over the next two to five years to achieve the vision in keeping with the shared purpose.

Chapter 9: Is it "Good Enough"?

Chapter 9 presents the *good-enough standard* for evaluating a given decision and determining whether consensus has been reached. Consensus requires an affirmative answer to four questions:

1. Is it right for me individually?
2. Is it right for the owner group and the family?
3. Will it work for the business and for the core capital as a whole?
4. Is it feasible in the real world?

The good-enough standard helps participants to analyze a given decision from multiple perspectives, and can help them pinpoint areas of concern that merit further discussion.

Chapter 10: Alternatives to Engaged Ownership

Chapter 10 discusses alternatives to engaged ownership. Not all owners will want to be engaged owners. They may be unable to reach consensus on shared purpose or vision for the future. If the majority of the group is willing, interested, and able to take on the work of engagement, but some are not, then there are two options that would enable the group to move forward: exit or delegation. If a larger part of the group is unwilling or unable to take on the work of developing consensus around shared purpose and vision, or the work itself generates disagreement that the group feels is insurmountable, then they will need to consider a different set of options. These include pruning the tree, dividing into silos, dividing the business through spinoff, splitoff, or splitup, or sale of the business.

Part III: Practicing Engaged Ownership

Part III lays out the practice of engaged ownership, and how owners do the work of developing and maintaining engagement.

Chapter 11: Forums

Chapter 11 discusses the purpose and benefits of creating forums for decision making. Each of the groups—family, owners, board, and management—has its own objectives and perspective. One of the responsibilities of the owners as the ultimate owners of the core capital is to create opportunities for each group's voice to be heard. Decision making for the business and core capital will be more effective if each group has a forum in which to come together to discuss the particular topics and issues that concern them.

Chapter 12: Allocating Power among Owners, Board, and Management

Chapter 12 discusses the challenge of allocating decision-making power among owners, board, and management, and in some cases the wider family.

All decision-making power within a corporation initially belongs to the owners. Statutes and codes governing business entities provide a default allocation of decision-making power, but also offer opportunities for very different allocations and thereby permit customized structures for reallocating decision-making power in ways that might better suit the needs of a particular family and business. At one end of the spectrum, the owners can retain all powers and control all decisions, which is the model seen in very small one-person businesses. Founder-run or controlling-owner businesses typically exhibit some degree of delegation to a board and management, but retain considerable power in the hands of the controlling owner. At the other end of the spectrum, owners can delegate most powers and choose to be relatively passive.

For engaged owners who have articulated a shared purpose and vision, and have begun the work of creating forums for family, business, and ownership discussion and decision making, the task is to allocate decision-making power in a way that gives the owners a voice in the highest level of strategic decision making, and the family a voice in issues that affect them, while still giving the board and management leeway to operate the business.

This chapter then presents a method for creating an allocation grid to permit the owners to allocate decision-making power among the groups and/or their forums.

Chapter 13: Working with Other Forums

Chapter 13 discusses the benefits and challenges of inter-forum meetings and decision making. Engaged owners don't operate in a vacuum. Their work is intended to guide the work of the board and management and to take into account the needs and wishes of the wider family.

An active and inviting Family Assembly can be a tremendous asset for a family and for engaged owners of a family business, because it can achieve respect as the voice of the family. When the Owners Council needs information and guidance about the family's wishes and needs, a strong Family Assembly with respected leadership will be trusted by the family to represent its interests promptly and accurately.

While the Family Assembly may be an entirely new forum, the business most likely already has a Board of Directors with well-established practices and a working relationship with management. The task, then, for the Owners Council is to introduce itself, the shared purpose, and the vision in a way that promotes dialog and collaboration with the board.

Chapter 14: Meetings

Chapter 14 describes how forum meetings can be scheduled, organized, and conducted to ensure that decision making is timely, thoughtful, and well-considered. The quality of forum decision making depends on the quality of the meetings that precede the decision.

Frequency: Meetings should be held often enough for the group to build the rapport, knowledge, and decision-making skills to do the forum's work effectively.

Meeting guidelines: A well-run meeting is scheduled well in advance and has a clear agenda. Materials are sent out in advance. Participants accept and adhere to a code of conduct.

Quorum and proxies: The group may choose to require a quorum for decision making and may or may not permit proxies.

Agendas: An agenda sets boundaries and manages participant expectations for the meeting. The chair of the forum may want to consider establishing an agenda cycle at least for the first several years of the forum's existence to ensure that the forum's members are educated on relevant topics and prepared to make the decisions for which they are responsible.

Participation: A forum may operate on a members-only basis or it may choose to invite presenters, participants, and/or observers.

Chapter 15: Policies

Chapter 15 discusses policies. A policy sets forth a decision agreed upon by two or more of the forums or provides the parameters within which a decision will be made, thereby providing guidance and helping to manage expectations of the groups vis-a-vis each other. Policies encourage a degree of consistency in decision making and promote investment by groups in long-range thinking and planning. When a policy is under development, it can be helpful for the participating forums to establish a joint task force to develop a draft of the policy.

Policies are living agreements. It is important to review policies from time to time to ensure that they continue to serve the purposes for which they were established. Major changes in circumstances all warrant prompt review of existing policies to ensure that they remain appropriate and effective.

Part IV: Three Challenges: Hats, Trusts, and Outside Investors

Part IV discusses three common situations that can challenge owners' efforts at developing engagement.

Chapter 16: When an Owner Also Runs the Enterprise

Chapter 16 discusses the challenges that can arise when an owner also runs the business. A managing owner's multiple roles may make it more difficult to reach consensus around shared purpose and vision with other owners and the risk of conflict among them may increase. A founder not only builds a business, he creates a culture and an established pattern of decision making around business issues. A child who succeeds the founder in running the business can find it difficult to make decisions together with other family members who own shares but don't work in the business, because these non-managing owners don't have the same level of information about the business or even a common vocabulary. Furthermore, joint decision making around ownership issues often simply isn't part of the culture of the business. To bring a managing owner into conversation with non-managing owners, it can help to begin with a group discussion. Issues that may be particularly challenging include: articulating a shared purpose and vision, allocating decision-making power in a new way, determining compensation and dividends, and redeploying core capital outside the business. The process of building owner engagement can help a managing owner develop a better understanding of and appreciation for the challenges of ownership, which are substantively different from the challenges of business management.

Chapter 17: When an Owner Is Also a Trustee

Chapter 17 describes the challenges to engaged ownership when the owners include a trustee. When a trust owns shares in a family business, ownership decision making must accommodate a fiduciary perspective. A trustee of a trust that owns shares has obligations to the beneficiaries that circumscribe the trustee's ownership choices. To operate effectively, the structure, membership, goals, and tasks of the Owners Council will need to take into account the purpose of the trust and the roles of the trustee and beneficiaries. Understanding the purpose of the trust will help determine the membership as well as goals and tasks of the Owners Council. To fulfill fiduciary obligations, the trustee will need to understand the needs and interests of the beneficiaries so that the trustee can factor that information into ownership decision making. The Owners Council can be a useful forum for gathering and disseminating information and for building rapport and mutual understanding between the trustee and the beneficiaries.

Where ownership of the business includes individuals as well as trusts, or includes separate trusts for different branches of a large family, it may be useful to create one or more Beneficiaries Assemblies. A Beneficiaries Assembly is tasked with educating the beneficiaries about the trust and providing an ongoing forum for trustee–beneficiary discussion.

Chapter 18: Bringing in Outside Investors

Chapter 18 discusses the impact on the owners, the family, and the business of bringing in an outside investor. Whereas the family owners have a shared interest in the human capital of the business and the wider family and an appreciation of the human and enterprise capital that make up their shared legacy, an outside investor is primarily concerned about a financial investment. An outside investor will be motivated to make decisions that enhance that investment and will have less concern for nonfinancial interests. An outside investor will want extensive information about the business and its financial and strategic plans. Family owners who are focused on core capital rather than liquidity and return on equity may find it difficult to find common ground with an outside owner while family owners who are less engaged may find that the demands of outside owners disturb the peaceful balance of power that has existed heretofore. Engaged owners will want to have an open discussion with the board about the advantages and disadvantages before bringing in outside capital to fund expansion or acquisitions. The Owners Council will want to perform extensive due diligence regarding the investor beforehand. The Owners Council may choose to restructure to accommodate the participation of the investor in ownership decision making.

***

Engaged Ownership offers family business owners a path to engagement with management, board, and family on the critical questions facing the business and the core capital. It also offers an alternative paradigm to more traditional models of family business governance. The process of engagement described here has enabled many family businesses to navigate ownership transitions over generations and to assess and deploy their core capital more thoughtfully. To family business owners reading this book, I hope that the ideas presented here will resonate with you and help you to articulate your vision and to invest every form of your core capital toward its highest and best use.

July 29, 2015

Acknowledgments

After starting my professional career as a lawyer, I have had the luck and privilege to learn my second and third professions, business management and consulting, on the job from two of the finest tutors possible: my father, J. S. Renkert, and Ken McCracken. With the rare privilege of a tutorial education comes a challenge: I do not always know the source of knowledge I gleaned. With apologies at the outset that I will omit many who deserve commendation for bringing clarity and nuance to the complex subject that is family business, my deep thanks to Ernesto Poza, Rob Kauer, Barbara Murray, Katherine McCarthy, Guy Renkert, Bill Cranshaw, Amy Malsin, Deidre O'Byrne, Edgar Schein, John Davis, John Ward, Craig Aronoff, Marion McCollom Hampton, Kelin Gersick, Ivan Lansberg, Dennis Jaffe, Don Opatrny, Bonnie Brown Hartley, Holly Isdale, Tom Davidow, F.C. Howland, Stuart Grodd, the entire team at Withers, attorneys for family held enterprises, and the Family Firm Institute, and to my most visionary teachers: our clients.

PART

I

Engaged Ownership: An Introduction

Prologue

Owen Family—January 3, 2010

Early in the morning, Charlie Owen went for a run. There was a board meeting coming up, and he suspected his two outside directors might ask him about succession planning. He had just signed estate planning documents two weeks ago, at the insistence of his wife, Ali, his daughter, Amanda, and his accountant. The estate plan wasn't exactly what he wanted, but it at least got everyone off his back. Ali had urged him to consider putting his 75 percent of the Owen Products' shares in trust, just as his uncle Fred had done, particularly since three of their four children had married and there would be less risk of the shares passing out of the family in the event of a divorce if the shares were held in trust. Charlie usually followed his wife's advice, particularly when it came to legal matters, but he couldn't imagine how he could have dealt with a trustee on top of everything else had his own father put the shares in trust, so he opted for the shares to pass to his children at his death instead. As for the taxes that would be due when he died and the shares passed, they would be paid for by insurance—thank goodness he didn't smoke and had the heart of an ox from all the marathon training. Ali would receive their house and Charlie's savings and investment accounts. Son Mike could run the company, drawing on his siblings for advice and support. Daughter Martha's husband, Ryan Jones, the head of operations for Owen Products West, could help. As he started up the long hill behind the football stadium, Charlie made himself a mental reminder to begin talking with Mike next week. Ali had suggested that Charlie call a family meeting to explain his plans. But was it really a good idea to talk about all this? What if the kids—or worse, their spouses—didn't agree with his plans?

Charlie was nearly to the top of the hill, still in full stride, when the pain hit. A motorist coming up the hill behind him saw him stumble, then collapse. She pulled over and ran to help, calling the emergency number on her mobile phone.

July 10, 2010

Meet the Owen family (Figure I.1). Charlie Owen took over the reins of Owen Products, Ltd., in 1975 from his father, John Owen, who founded the company in 1948. Like his father, Charlie was a driven businessman, and as a result of his efforts over four decades Owen Products is now a leading manufacturer of clay pots for the domestic greenhouse industry. The company has two manufacturing facilities, Owen Products East and Owen Products West. Each serves a distinct market due to the very different climates on either side of the country. Owen Products East primarily serves greenhouses in the East, where it is wet and cool. Eastern greenhouses want pots that can withstand freeze–thaw conditions so that they can be used outside. Owen Products West primarily serves greenhouses in the West, where it is hot and dry. Western greenhouses want pots that can withstand extreme heat and will absorb and retain water, thus reducing the amount of watering that must be done to keep the plants healthy. Owen Products has developed distinct technologies in each of its

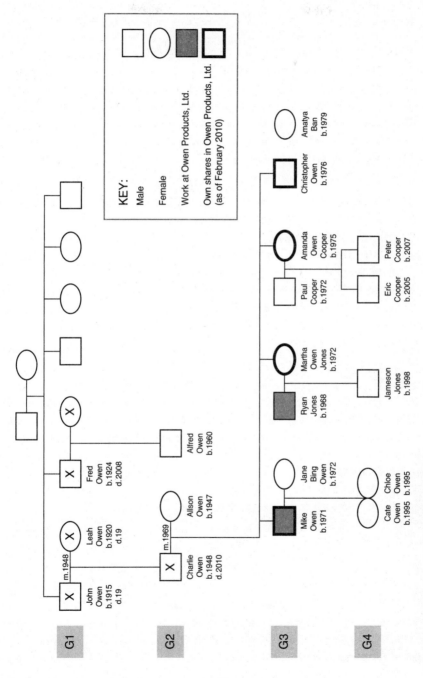

Figure I.1 Owen Family Tree (as of February 2010)

KEY:

Male

Female

Work at Owen Products, Ltd.

Own shares in Owen Products, Ltd.
(as of February 2010)

G1

John
Owen
b.1915
d.19

m.1948

Leah
Owen
b.1920
d.19

Fred
Owen
b.1924
d.2008

G2

Charlie
Owen
b.1948
d.2010

m.1969

Allson
Owen
b.1947

Alfred
Owen
b.1960

G3

Mike
Owen
b.1971

Jane
Bing
Owen
b.1972

Ryan
Jones
b.1968

Martha
Owen
Jones
b.1972

Paul
Cooper
b.1972

Amanda
Owen
Cooper
b.1975

Christopher
Owen
b.1976

Amatya
Ban
b.1979

G4

Cate
Owen
b.1995

Chloe
Owen
b.1995

Jameson
Jones
b.1998

Eric
Cooper
b.2005

Peter
Cooper
b.2007

5

manufacturing facilities to meet the needs of greenhouses on both sides of the country. The company makes pots in thousands of different sizes and shapes, including custom sizes for top customers. It also prides itself on quick and accurate deliveries to its biggest greenhouse customers and has made a substantial investment in supply chain and logistics management technology. As a result, Owen Products' clay pots command a higher price in the marketplace than their competition.

Charlie Owen died six months ago, leaving his shares (representing 75% of the outstanding shares of Owen Products, Ltd.) to his four children:

1. Mike Owen, born 1971, now president, formerly served as vice president of sales for Owen Products East.
2. Martha Owen Jones, born 1972, homemaker, is married to Ryan Jones, VP of operations for Owen Products West.
3. Amanda Owen Cooper, born 1975, is an attorney who practices with a corporate law firm in the West.
4. Christopher Owen, born 1976, is an associate professor of applied mathematics at Eastern University.

The remaining 25 percent of the shares are held in a trust that was created by Charlie's Uncle Fred for the benefit of his son, Alfred, who suffers from severe cerebral palsy (Figure I.2). Fred was Owen Products' CFO for more than 40 years. Fred died in 2008 and named Charlie as trustee of the trust for Alfred. Charlie named his daughter, Amanda, as successor trustee. Dividends from the

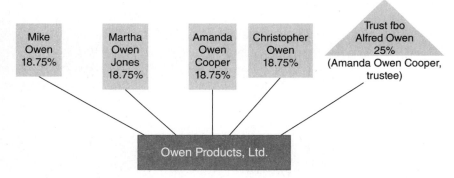

Figure I.2   Owen Products, Ltd. Ownership Chart

shares are expected to provide much of the funding for Alfred's ongoing care.

Charlie's death was unexpected; a self-described health-food "nut" and marathon runner, he collapsed one day during a training session and never regained consciousness. Doctors told his wife, Alison, that he had suffered from an undetected aneurysm.

The board of Owen Products, Ltd. (Mike, Alison, the company's outside general counsel, the owner of a prominent Eastern greenhouse, and a local professor of botany) named Mike as president and CEO.

The Owen kids are proud to be the third generation of shareholders of Owen Products, and they are excited about the opportunities they see in the clay pot industry. As Charlie told them from the time they were small, "People will always want potted plants, and terra cotta is the best possible pot for growing them." But the Owen children are finding that there is no roadmap for the journey they have embarked on. While they have always enjoyed close relationships, they find themselves disagreeing on seemingly simple decisions.

The business isn't running smoothly; employee complaints are increasing, cash flow is slowing, and major customers have suggested they may turn to other suppliers. The board, which previously served primarily as a sounding board for Charlie, isn't accustomed to strategic planning, and they have proven to be little help as Mike tries to navigate his new role. Their advisors are telling Mike that he should buy out his siblings. Martha, Amanda, and Christopher are beginning to question Mike's motives.

A major competitor called to ask whether they would consider selling the business "now that Charlie is gone." Mike, offended, slammed down the phone. When Mike joked about the call at a family gathering, Amanda was shocked and scolded him for not bringing the offer to the board and shareholders.

Martha and her husband, Ryan, want to bring their son, Jameson, into the company when he graduates from university; Amanda (whose children are much younger) is worried about "equal opportunities."

Christopher called Mike recently to ask when the dividend would be paid, and whether he could expect an increase next year. Mike has been avoiding Christopher since then.

The Owen children, as the controlling owners of Owen Products, Ltd., feel as though they are alone in uncharted territory. But the Owen children are not alone—in fact, the situation they face is increasingly common. What is happening here? What can they do about it? How can they come together to lead Owen Products forward? And why does much of the advice they are receiving seem off-base?

A Note about the Owens and Owen Products, Ltd.

Readers whose involvement in a family business revolves around very different sorts of companies—larger, more international, more technology- or service-oriented—may wonder whether the Owens' story and this book will be relevant to them. In family business there are certain patterns that recur over and over, regardless of setting. This book focuses on one of those patterns: a group of related individuals inherit shares of a family business that previously was controlled and managed by a single person, and struggle to find their place within the business system. This book focuses on a relatively small family in a relatively old and slow-to-change industry to illustrate these patterns, so as to minimize the business-oriented distractions that might otherwise arise in the telling.

This is not a story about dysfunction. The Owen children are intelligent, educated, well-adjusted, and capable adults with good jobs, adequate financial resources outside the business, and a strong commitment to family and their family business. Certainly, they share the challenges that most families face—raising children, dealing with an aging mother who now finds herself widowed, and managing complex professions, growing financial obligations, and busy family lives. But in the main, the Owens are as well-prepared to be owners of a business as anyone. The Owens are entirely fictitious, but they are similar to many business-owning families. The challenges they face in becoming engaged owners of Owen Products, Ltd. do not arise from their interpersonal relationships as family members, but rather from their new relationship to the company and the family's core capital. They will not be able to resolve those conflicts simply by relating better to each other (though good communications skills will certainly stand them in good stead). Rather, dealing with those conflicts will require that the Owens get organized in an entirely new way, by developing structures and policies that will enable them to look at capital and strategy at the highest level and support them in developing a new decision-making structure and allocation of power among the owners, board, and management.

1

More at Stake than Money

Refocusing the Succession Planning Discussion

Refocus the discussion around business succession planning from who's going to run the company to what is the best use of the core capital.

News stories about family business disputes are eternally popular because they have all the elements of epic tragedy: love, greed, betrayal, loss. Readers know how the plot will turn out: owners can't agree on the future of the business; they take their disagreement to court; a lengthy and public battle ensues; a fortune is spent on the battle; the business is lost and the family is torn apart.

Often, blame for this tragic ending is laid squarely on the family owners. They only wanted big dividends. They fought each other for control. They couldn't agree on whether to sell the business. They failed to change course before disaster struck. Certainly, there are plenty of examples of such behavior. So often are owners cast in the role of villain that advisors to family businesses regularly suggest that ownership and control should be concentrated in the hands of a single individual, to avoid conflict that could arise when family members with different viewpoints, needs, and agendas share ownership of a business.

This book takes a different perspective on family business ownership. How can family owners be the core strength of the business, and not the villains? How can owners be the source of a unified and thoughtful vision for the future? How can they be engaged in an ongoing, productive conversation with family, board, and management, strengthening the long-term value of the business, the family's core capital and the owners' stake in it?

To see family business ownership in this new light, we need to think differently about the roles and responsibilities of family owners, their shared purpose, and their collective vision for the future. We need to refocus the discussion around business succession planning from *who's going to run the company?* to *what is the best use of the core capital?*

By definition, owners of a business own the equity capital—the value that would remain if the business and its assets were sold, and all its debts and other obligations paid in full. That definition underlies most economic and business theory. But that definition of what exactly is owned, while useful for accounting and financial purposes, is uncomfortably limiting when the business in question has been owned by a family over generations.

The core capital of a family business has been built over generations and reflects the contributions and efforts of many different people.

If a group of family owners were to sit down together for a while and talk about what exactly they own, they might come up with a longer list, one that included many different kinds of capital:

- *Financial capital:* money and equivalents; the income and distributions from the business; the financial value of physical assets such as equipment, raw materials, inventories, and real estate.
- *Human and social capital:* their individual and family relationships; their talents; drive, perseverance, grit and determination; their strongly held values and their entrepreneurial zeal; the formal and informal education they've received, and the experience and knowledge base they hold individually and as a group; the family's relationships and connections; its values; the reservoir of goodwill and their good name, within the family, the business, and the wider community.

- *Enterprise capital:* unique knowhow; combinations of financial and human capital unique to the family and its business, which generate a return greater than what the separate elements would generate individually; the societal value of the product or service the business provides.

This is the core capital of a family and its business—a different, broader, more encompassing view of what it is that the owners of the business in fact own. Some of the core capital is related to the business activities of the business; some is related to the unique personality, culture, and values of the family that created it; and some is a result of the synergy of family and business together. The core capital has been built over one or more generations and reflects the contributions and efforts of many. The core capital also reflects withdrawals and reductions that may have occurred due to mistakes, failed efforts, lack of attention, external events such as market changes, wars, or recessions, strategic choices, withdrawals, sales, deaths, feuds, or exits. In a legal sense, the owners "own" only the financial capital. But they are responsible for the human capital and the enterprise capital as well, because they have the power and the responsibility to make the ultimate decisions—keep, sell, expand, contract, invest, leverage, harvest—that will have decisive impact on the future of the human capital and the enterprise capital.

Every group of owners will assess and value their core capital differently, just as they will determine their financial risk–reward calculus differently. They will also reassess and revalue from time to time, as owners join and leave the group, and as their circumstances, environment, and perspective change. There is no absolute standard; for a privately held business, what is important is that the owners agree on what constitutes their core capital and how they will measure performance.

Focusing on financial capital alone—measuring results solely with a financial yardstick—may well result in human or enterprise capital being misused or wasted.

One of the basic tenets of investing is that capital should be invested—if it just sits passively, it risks going to waste. This is true of every kind of core capital invested—not just financial capital.

Focusing on financial capital alone—measuring results solely with a financial yardstick—may well result in human or enterprise capital being misused or wasted. If the human capital includes excellent community relationships, then moving the business to maximize financial profits may destroy the relationship with the community. If the enterprise capital includes superb customer service, automating those processes could hurt morale and performance. All forms of capital come together to drive results, and focusing on nonfinancial core capital can help owners to recognize the full extent of the value their ownership represents. So, who is tasked with watching over core capital of a family business?

The premise of this book is that owners—not the board, not management—are ultimately responsible for overseeing the deployment of the financial, human, and enterprise capital. They alone have the interest, perspective, and responsibility to determine their shared purpose, their vision for the future of the business, and the yardsticks by which they will measure return on core capital and, ultimately, success.

Owners have this responsibility precisely because they are the holders of the residual core capital—their capital is what would remain if the business were sold or shut its doors. In the end, only they can determine what is an acceptable risk or a desirable return. Only they can decide if the potential rewards of being in a given business activity offset the risks, and, if not, how the core capital should be redeployed.

This book is a handbook for current and future family owners who recognize the unique value of the core capital invested in their family businesses and who wish to play a more active role in overseeing how that core capital is used, invested, and reinvested over time. It presents a paradigm for family owners—engaged ownership—and lays out how they can create more effective partnerships with family, board, and management to ensure the long-term sustainability and growth of core capital. The key to engaged ownership is clarifying the roles and relationships of owners to the other groups in the business—board, management, and family—and then organizing themselves to promote effective decision making on the critical matters for which the owners bear responsibility, and working effectively with board, management, and family.

Part II lays out the process by which a group of owners can achieve engaged ownership of their family business. First, owners consider the legacy they have inherited, and the attitudes and assumptions around ownership that have been passed down along with the business. Then, by enumerating their core capital and articulating their shared purpose as owners, they develop a richer understanding of their core capital and its role in the business and the family. By defining their vision for the future, they establish the highest level objectives for board and management. But not all family owners are willing or able to become engaged owners, and Part II also discusses viable alternatives to engaged ownership.

Part III provides on-the-job guidance for engaged owners. Owners don't operate in a vacuum, and Part III delineates the process by which engaged owners can establish an Owners Council as the forum for their work as owners. Part III then considers the allocation of decision-making power among owners, board, and management, and the importance of building engagement with the board and with the broader family. It provides advice and guidance on setting the meeting agenda and operating forum meetings. Part III ends with a discussion of policies and the value of defining the boundaries of forum decision making on key topics such as distributions and redemptions, family employment, privacy and confidentiality, and compensation.

Part IV considers the challenges for ownership decision making when the ownership group faces three very different ownership constellations:

1. When family owners also manage the company
2. When the ownership group includes trustees of shareholder trusts
3. When the ownership group includes non-family investors who are not related to the family who founded the business

What these three ownership constellations have in common is that these owners will have very strong and distinct perspectives and objectives as a result of their other roles that may make it much more difficult for them to reach consensus around shared purpose and vision with other owners. Part IV helps engaged owners understand these constellations, consider their implications, and make decisions more effectively.

Owen Family—March 7, 1948

Owen Products was founded in 1948 by John Owen. John had returned from the War in 1946. He longed to get away from battle and return to his family's small farm in the east. The war had interrupted his education, and he planned to finish his engineering degree at the local university as quickly as possible. But upon his return, he found that his father, a kiln fireman in a clay drainage pipe factory, was gravely ill and his mother was struggling to care for John's younger sisters and brother. John put aside his plans to return to university and instead got a job at the same clay pipe factory where his father had worked. Construction was booming after the War, driving demand for clay drainage pipe, and the factory was operating at capacity. The discipline, focus, and maturity that John had acquired during the War led to frequent promotions. John soon found himself working as the afternoon kiln fireman under the watchful tutelage of the kiln supervisor, David Smith.

The eastern region had plentiful clay deposits, and the clay used by the pipe factory was of a variety particularly well-suited to the manufacture of drainage pipes, being able to withstand kiln firing at higher temperatures. David Smith was a scientist at heart and he found John Owen to be a quick study. David spent time showing John how the clay behaved when mixed with other clays in various blends and fired at different temperatures and for different lengths of time. David pointed out that the longer the firing time, and the higher the firing temperature, the less porous the resulting pipe would be. David also commented that the eastern clays were also adaptable to firing for shorter cycle times and lower temperatures, resulting in a more porous pipe, but one that was equally strong. John enjoyed his impromptu ceramics lessons and had many ideas for how the clay pipe-forming process could be streamlined, but he found the job frustrating because the head of manufacturing had no interest in listening to his and David Smith's ideas.

In late January 1948, the owner of a small commercial greenhouse down the road visited the clay pipe factory. A local pottery had long supplied his greenhouse with terra cotta pots, but the potter had just died with no heirs and the pottery was being shuttered. Could the clay pipe factory also manufacture greenhouse pots? The owner of the clay pipe factory was sympathetic, but the kilns were full and there was no room for additional product to be fired. John, overhearing the conversation, mentioned the opportunity to David Smith. David's response surprised John—he said the pottery had the best clay pit in the region and, if its presses and kilns were modernized and expanded, could be a leading clay pot manufacturer. David urged John to talk with the potter's widow, who might be willing to sell the pottery.

John went home after his shift with his head swirling with ideas. Should he consider going into business? Could he support his mother and siblings? Might David Smith be willing to come and work with him? Would his fiancée, Leah, be willing to have a smaller wedding so that they could get the pottery up and running?

Owen Family—October 31, 1968

John and Leah Owen threw a big party in the old pottery to celebrate the twentieth anniversary of Owen Products, Ltd. The old mixers and presses, outdated now, provided a rustic backdrop in contrast to the white linen–dressed tabletops, decorated with clay pots of all shapes and sizes filled with blooming flowers and trailing ivy. Everyone—suppliers, customers, bankers, friends, and neighbors—had come to celebrate Owen Products' hard-earned success. In his speech to his guests, John made a few jokes about the "rough years" but spent most of his time saluting his partner and closest friend, David Smith, who had left the comfortable safety of the clay pipe plant to join John in the new venture back in 1948, and the contributions of his younger brother, Fred, who had joined Owen Products in 1955 after finishing his accountancy training. John didn't say anything about the kiln explosion in 1959 that had destroyed the first manufacturing building and nearly leveled the small warehouse next door. Nor did he mention the rough patch in the early 1960s, when his former employer, the clay pipe factory, decided to branch out into clay greenhouse pots after plastic drainage pipe became the industry standard. Through it all, Owen Products had survived. One by one, the guests stood to toast John Owen and his company.

Standing to the side and listening to his father's speech and the guests' toasts, Charlie Owen thought about all his father had accomplished. Owen Products was considered one of the best places to work in town, because John paid a fair wage and he liked to help hardworking employees take on new challenges and advance their careers. The pots that Owen Products made were simple, in the larger scheme of things, but more complex than they appeared; John Owen had always invested in the best grinding, forming, and firing technology Owen Products could buy, always plowing profits back into the business. Owen Products stood by its greenhouse customers, committed to shipping on time and sometimes accepting late payment, especially during the late winter when greenhouses were building inventory for the springtime rush. Charlie knew that his mother, Leah, had also been an important factor in Owen Products' success; it had been she who had persuaded the potter's widow to sell John the pottery in the first place, in exchange for John's small savings, a promissory note, and (to John's dismay) the proceeds from selling her grandmother's diamond ring. She took an interest in the employees—she knew everyone's name and, when she visited the plant, asked about their families. Charlie, their only child, knew that John and Leah had wanted a big family; in many ways, the company had become the second child for both of them, carefully nurtured and brought to adulthood.

Charlie also thought about the future of Owen Products. Charlie, like his father, had enjoyed a decade working alongside David Smith, learning about the properties of the flexible eastern clays when fired at different temperatures and firing curves. He had recently returned from a yearlong graduate program at Western University. The western part of the country was in the eighth year of drought, and water rationing requirements were challenging farmers and greenhouses. Charlie had met with greenhouse owners during his time there and asked David whether Owen Products' eastern clays might be mixed with western riverbed clays to produce a lightweight pot porous enough to soak up water and release it slowly while still remaining strong. He and David had shipped in samples of the riverbed clays and had been experimenting with various blends. Charlie was cautiously optimistic that they had found the right blend; he planned to ship samples of the pots to one of his greenhouse operator friends out west next week.

Charlie was glad to see that his uncle Fred, the controller for Owen Products, had brought his son Alfred to the party. Fred was John's youngest brother, and he had been with the business almost since its founding. Alfred, who suffered from cerebral palsy and was unable to walk, sat in his new wheelchair, a gift from John and Leah last year. Fred was a widower, and he raised Alfred on his own. John believed that one of Owen Products' responsibilities was to serve as a safety net for family members, and he and Leah took particular care to make sure Alfred had the care he needed.

Charlie was startled out of his musings by an elbow to the ribs—his fiancée, Alison, brought him back to reality, as she always did. "Time to dance with me, Charlie-boy!" Charlie had met Ali at Western University, where she was studying corporate law. Ali was a wild Bohemian on the surface but a scholar at heart—so different from the eastern girls Charlie had dated before. Charlie was smitten. On top of everything else, Ali understood the complex water use laws being adopted by western legislators in response to the long drought, and had helped Charlie understand the opportunities that the western region offered to a manufacturer that could make pots that were light and porous but strong. Her family was in the retail business, and Ali told Charlie that small, family-owned greenhouses were being bought up by consolidators across the West. Small customers were disappearing in the West—could Owen Products increase supply and lower costs enough to meet the demands of a multinational chain of growers?

Owen Family—March 12, 1986

The year 1986 brought the best of times and the worst of times for Charlie Owen. He and Ali, who had married in 1970 and welcomed four children over the following decade, watched proudly as their oldest son, Michael, helped his team win the local football championship. Owen Products opened a new manufacturing facility in the West, focused on serving the western grower chains. Leah Owen, who had been the spirit of Owen Products for nearly 40 years, now battled Parkinson's disease. And David Smith, a smoker for many years, was diagnosed with advanced lung cancer. Charlie's father, John Owen, was worried about his wife and closest friend and focused on them more and more, leaving operations to Charlie. It was exhilarating and terrifying in equal measure: Charlie found himself traveling constantly between East and West, struggling to manage payroll and debt payments, negotiating with new clients, tweaking clay body mixes and firing curves in David Smith's absence. Ali had taken an indefinite leave of absence from her job at a prominent eastern law firm when Michael was born. She had not returned; though she missed the law, she felt she could contribute more to the family staying home. With Charlie traveling constantly, she had her hands full.

Owen Family—December 24, 1992

Charlie hurried through the Owen Products East plant. He had yet to finish his holiday shopping; he hoped that Ali had (as usual) bought some extra gifts and picked something nice out for herself besides. He was bone tired and looking forward to some quiet time with his family—not that there were all that many quiet times with four children, especially with Michael and Martha home from college. Not having grown up with siblings, Charlie was sometimes at a loss when his daughters squabbled about boyfriends or his youngest, Christopher, shut himself away for hours. At least Mike seemed familiar—he was a reasonably good student, athletic, well-liked, and enjoyed all the same things Charlie had liked at his age.

Charlie was looking forward to seeing his uncle, Fred, at the family dinner. Now that both his parents were gone, Charlie had grown closer to his uncle. Fred was now chief financial officer for Owen Products, and always listened willingly when Charlie brought a worry or a quandary about the financial side of the business. Charlie knew that Owen Products needed to upgrade its accounting systems; he told Ali he was unwilling to disturb his uncle's routines but, really, he wanted to buy some time before taking on yet another big expense. He felt the same way about dividends—before John died last year, he had counseled Charlie that when he inherited John's 75 percent and became majority shareholder, Charlie should consider implementing a dividend policy that would ease Fred's impending retirement and provide for Alfred's care. Charlie saw the wisdom in his father's advice, but so far had done nothing—there just wasn't enough cash to meet all the demands, it seemed. Besides, Fred was making a decent salary, so perhaps dividends could wait. The western plant had proven out his father's old adage, "Takes longer, costs more," and Charlie was still struggling to perfect technical specifications, product design, and pricing for the western market. Ali had been correct in her predictions that the small greenhouses would be consolidated, but Charlie hadn't been prepared for just how difficult and demanding the major growers would be. Furthermore, the West was enjoying the wettest decade on record and the major growers were turning their attention to lighter, more decorative pots now that porosity and water retention were less critical. Owen Products was making money, but not much. Dividends would need to wait.

CHAPTER 2

Achieving Engaged Ownership

Engaged ownership is a group effort: it takes collaboration on the part of the owners, and communication among those playing the key roles in the business—owners, board, management, and family.

Engaged ownership is a group effort: it takes collaboration on the part of the owners, and communication among those playing the key roles in the business—owners, board, management, and family. Engagement can't happen on paper—it requires face-to-face discussion, dialog, and debate. This is because core capital is finite; there is simply not enough core capital to accomplish every goal that every participant envisions. So, it is understandable that those in each role have strongly held but conflicting perspectives and priorities about how it should be deployed. Owners, as the ultimate owners of the core capital, need to come to consensus and articulate their shared purpose and vision for the deployment of their core capital; in turn, family, board, and management need opportunities to understand the owners' vision and to offer comments and questions and raise their own perspectives on matters of concern. (And if there isn't some degree of disagreement, dialog, and debate, something is probably missing in the process.)

Owners must organize and lead the work to achieve engagement. This is not a process that the board or management can orchestrate. Once the owners decide to do the work to accomplish engagement, they will need to devote time and attention to it on a regular basis. Acting together as owners takes time, effort, and practice. As with taking on any new discipline, the important thing is to begin; owners will find engagement begins to improve almost immediately, and will continue to build so long as the owners attend to the process.

It isn't necessary to engage a facilitator to guide the owners through the work of engagement, but having a facilitator in the room can make the process flow more smoothly. For a small group, or for a controlling owner who plays all the major roles in the business, the facilitator can serve as springboard for discussion, goad, critical thinker, and/or Socratic questioner. For a large group, the facilitator can manage the process to ensure everyone has an opportunity to speak and be heard, and to minimize the risk that debate will spiral into anger and frustration. The facilitator can also keep track of the group's responses and areas of agreement and disagreement and help to set agendas to deal with ongoing issues.

When?

> When there is major disagreement among owners about the future course of the business, working to increase engagement can help the owners achieve a better understanding of their individual and collective visions for the future and choose a course of action.

Owners can begin the work of engagement any time. Typically, owners will want to undertake the work of developing engagement when circumstances have changed and the natural governance system—"the way we do things around here"—no longer keeps the business in a comfortable equilibrium. The owners may find themselves frustrated by a lack of common purpose with those who run the company. They may feel that they have no way to provide input, and sense they are stuck. Sometimes, the lack of alignment is between owners and management; sometimes it is among the owners themselves. When there is major disagreement among owners about the future course of the business, working to increase engagement can help the owners achieve a better understanding of their individual and collective visions for the future and choose a course of action.

It is particularly important for owners to come together in connection with a significant ownership transition. For example, adult children who inherit shares will need to begin to learn their new role as owners: enumerating their core capital, defining their shared purpose and vision, and developing relationships with others who hold key roles in the business, particularly if one or more of them also serve as directors or in management roles. Likewise, individuals who become trustees of trusts that own significant shares of the business will want to define their role vis-a-vis the business—as owner—and vis-a-vis the grantor and the beneficiaries—as trustee. And owners considering bringing in an outside investor will want to define their shared purpose and vision well before the transaction takes place so that they can determine whether the benefits of the transaction (such as generating liquidity for the group, or enabling an unhappy owner to exit) outweigh the potential drawbacks (such as changing policies around family employment or corporate charitable giving to meet the demands of the more financially oriented outside owner).

Core Capital

> Enumerating core capital is an exercise of thinking about all that has been invested in the business and the family over time—all the assets, in all forms, that make up their legacy and their future opportunity set.

To take on the responsibility of engaged ownership, owners first need to consider: What is the core capital of our business and our family? What is at stake?

For purposes of this book, we'll think about three forms of core capital[1]:

1. *Financial capital*: money and equivalents; the income and distributions from the business; the financial value of physical assets such as equipment, raw materials, inventories, and real estate
2. *Human capital*: the owners' individual and family relationships; the family's talents; drive, perseverance, grit and determination; their strongly held values and their entrepreneurial zeal; the formal and informal education

they've received, and the experience and knowledge base they hold individually and as a group; the family's relationships and connections; its influence, its values; the reservoir of goodwill and their good name, within the family, the business, and the wider community

3. *Enterprise capital:* innovations in research, design, product, service, process; combinations of capital unique to the family and its business that generate a return greater than what the separate elements would generate individually; the societal value of the product or service the business provides

No two families define their core capital the same way. Enumerating core capital is an exercise of thinking about all that has been invested in the business and the family over time—all the assets, in all forms, that make up their legacy and their future opportunity set.

Shared Purpose

Why do we want to be involved in this business (and the core capital it represents) together as owners—if at all?

The second step to engaged ownership is articulating a common shared purpose. The shared purpose is the answer to the question: *Why do we want to be involved in this business (and the core capital it represents) together as owners—if at all?* Without a shared purpose, there will not be enough "glue" to bond the owners to each other and to their collective investment. In the absence of a good enough shared purpose, there will be an increased risk of acrimony as owners seek different returns from the same business. This risk heightens the importance of thinking broadly about ownership of the core capital, rather than just the financial capital, of the business: each owner needs to understand how the others value the business and what is important to them. With a family business, there is almost always more at stake than money.

Ultimately, the shared purpose reflects a voluntary emotional commitment on the part of each owner to spend time with their fellow owners making important decisions that will affect their own and other people's lives, and the deployment of the core capital. The shared purpose of any ownership group will be unique and even idiosyncratic. Business success is generally part of the mix, but rarely do purely financial purposes (to generate above-average profits) top the list. Rather, the shared purpose draws together the core reasons this group remains in this specific business venture together.

Sometimes, owners conclude that they simply do not have a good enough shared purpose to want to stay together as owners. Each owner may be able to articulate a purpose, but they find there is no consensus among them. Those who focus on business continuity as the measure of family business success might deem this outcome failure; but why? If by recognizing their lack of shared purpose the group can make reasoned, dispassionate, and sensible decisions about how to move forward—whether to split up the business so parts can be run separately, sell it all, or redeem out one or more of the owners in a way that preserves as much of the core capital as possible and allocates capital among the owners in a way they agree upon—then such an outcome looks much more like success.

Vision

The vision is what the owners would describe as their "True North"—a description of the goals they are striving to achieve and the criteria they will use to measure their version of success.

The vision is what the owners would describe as their "True North"—a description of the goals they are striving to achieve and the criteria they will use to measure their version of success. This definition of *vision* points out why it is so important for the owners to do the work of articulating their vision: They must be able to explain to the board and management what is often a very unique and distinctive set of goals. If the owners don't do this work, the board might quite reasonably assume that the owners measure performance purely by financial metrics. Directors might substitute their own vision, or the vision of a public company in the same industry (for example, some board members might assume that owners would want fast growth, or a perfectly level dividend, or to be listed in the Forbes 100), when in fact the owners don't value those outcomes. Only if the owners do the work of articulating the vision will the board know what to work with management to aim for.

For some groups of owners, the vision may be couched primarily in financial terms and will put the financial capital foremost. For others, the vision will include goals that relate to non-financial forms of core capital. While most owners' vision typically will include some basic financial performance measures, it also will include some non-financial standards.

For the owners, these non-financial (or personal financial) goals are just as important as the financial goals. Some may have their basis in the family's history (such as an aversion to debt); others may reflect the owners' desire to right-size the business and their involvement; still others may reflect the family's view of its role in the community (however the family may define *community*). The vision may seem illogical to non-family members who focus primarily on profit, and the vision may indeed reduce profitability and/or free cash flow from what it would be if the goals were not pursued, but achieving the vision is critical to the owners.

When owners have strong non-financial shared purpose and vision, they must be able to articulate it, and have a role in setting high-level business goals, if they are to realize the vision.

Endnote

1. The concept that there are multiple forms of capital has come to be widely accepted. For a somewhat different but very useful perspective on the capital of a family enterprise, see Jay Hughes' *Family Wealth—Keeping it in the Family* (Wiley, 2004).

Owen Family—October 19, 1996

The year 1996 had been a momentous one for Owen Products, Ltd. Michael, now 26, took over sales for Owen Products East, giving Charlie more time to focus on the western business. Michael was steady and focused, Charlie felt; he didn't have his grandfather's scientific bent, or his mother's energy and insight, but he had a real talent for developing strong and lasting relationships with Owen Products' greenhouse customers. Michael's sister, Martha, had headed west for university and showed no signs of ever wanting to return. She had been an indifferent student but an enthusiastic leader of her sorority's community service program, so Charlie recruited her to manage the community service program he had instituted companywide to help employee families facing unexpected medical emergencies. Martha had inherited her grand-mother Leah's talent for meeting and befriending everyone in the plant; Charlie suspected that her interest in Ryan Jones, a manu-facturing supervisor fresh out of university, might in fact go a bit beyond friendship. Charlie worried about what might happen if one of his children were to marry an employee, but he pushed that issue to the back of his mind, spending nearly all his time dealing with the big western buyers. Besides, Ryan showed real talent, and perhaps a relationship with Martha might help keep him at Owen Products.

Amanda and Christopher were in graduate school, having demonstrated academic aptitude that surprised Charlie. He guessed that they would not follow their older siblings into the company, but would make their own way. Sometimes, Charlie wondered whether Amanda's desire to study law was an echo of her mother's interest that had been stymied when motherhood and Charlie's preoccupation with the business had cut short Ali's own legal career. Whether inherited or not, Amanda's aptitude for the law was real; she helped Charlie understand the legal implications of new environmental and product safety regulations applicable to their greenhouse clients but also frustrated him when she focused only on the legal side of an issue. Christopher, meanwhile, still puzzled Charlie. A bit of a loner, Christopher had proven himself to be eerily smart and focused his studies on advanced theoretical mathematics. Christopher showed little interest in the day-to-day happenings at the business and looked positively bored whenever dinner discussion turned to the company during his visits home.

Owen Family—March 13, 2008

It was a beautiful early spring day—one of those days when gardeners, tired of the long dark winter, survey their gardens and porches and head to the greenhouse, Charlie mused. He wished he, too, were gardening, or at least out for a run; instead, he stood with Ali and his children in the church doorway, shaking hands and embracing employees and friends. Charlie felt very alone, even with Ali and his children and their spouses by his side: his Uncle Fred, the retired chief financial officer at Owen Products, had died suddenly of a heart attack, and now no one was left of John Owen's generation. Charlie would miss Fred's dry sense of humor, his unending patience, and his excellent grasp of Owen Products' financials. Charlie had hired another CFO but felt he had never really been able to fill the hole Fred had left when he retired 12 years before. Fred's son, Alfred, wasn't at the church; the cold virus that was plaguing the East had hit Alfred hard. Wheelchair bound and with limited mobility due to cerebral palsy, Alfred struggled with respiratory problems, and now he had a serious case of bronchitis that was not responding well to antibiotics. Charlie felt a heavy weight; Fred had named him trustee of a trust that held Fred's 25 percent interest in Owen Products, for the benefit of Alfred, and Alfred's care was now squarely Charlie's responsibility.

3

Engaged Ownership: Hallmarks and Impediments

Interest, Understanding, Ability, Longsightedness/Broadsightedness

What are the hallmarks of an engaged owner?

Interest

An engaged owner is interested in the work of the business and the investment of the core capital represented by his ownership. He is willing to devote the time to attend scheduled meetings and participate in discussions around business issues. He reads materials provided by the board (and management) and also follows news about the industry, business in general, and family business in particular. He is mindful of all the forms of core capital and how they are deployed in the business.

Understanding

An engaged owner understands the owners' role and relationships, and the appropriate scope of her involvement. She takes care to raise issues and participate in discussions in the proper forum, and to postpone discussions that might pop up elsewhere (such as over a holiday dinner with family).

Ability

An engaged owner works to maintain her knowledge of general business, investments, and strategy so that she can evaluate options when decisions must be made. She knows what she doesn't know; she seeks input and advice from others as necessary. She has the time to devote to exercising ownership responsibilities. An engaged owner is able to listen actively to others and consider alternative viewpoints. She is able and willing to express her own ideas and ask tough and unpopular questions, but with tact and respect. She has the discipline and maturity to work with others toward a common vision even though there may be no immediate personal benefit to doing so.

Longsightedness/Broadsightedness

An engaged owner thinks about choices over the long term, and considers the broad implications of a decision. He thinks about choices several steps ahead, and about non-financial as well as financial consequences of a given decision. An engaged owner thinks about a future that is years and often generations ahead.

The key to becoming engaged owners is finding and voicing a shared purpose and a common vision for the future of the business and the core capital.

Is this definition of engaged ownership achievable? Yes, it is. The key to becoming engaged owners is finding and voicing a shared purpose and a common vision for the future of the business and the core capital. Owners find that the drive to become and remain engaged comes when they articulate a common shared purpose and recognize that they alone are ultimately responsible for the core capital deployed in the business, and that their work and decision making can meaningfully increase the odds that the core capital will be sustained over time.

In practice, engaged owners focus on three questions:

1. What is our core capital?
2. What is our shared purpose? Why do we choose to be owners of this business and our core capital together?

3. What is our vision? What exactly is our core capital, and what is the most productive way to deploy it going forward? How do we organize ourselves, the business, and the deployment of our core capital to achieve our shared purpose and our vision?

Several aspects of this list of questions are worth mentioning up front.

First, the owners own a business, but the questions have to do with the core capital. That is because the core capital includes the business but is broader than the business alone. A significant part of the core capital could continue to exist even if the business failed or the owners opted to expand, sell, or shutter it, or to create an entirely new and different business. For that reason, focusing on business-level decisions alone ("What is the future of this business?") is defining the question too narrowly.

Engaged ownership is a choice that must affirmatively be made by each individual owner—an owner cannot be an engaged owner against her will, or consider himself engaged but just come along for the ride.

Second, the questions hinge on the decision of a group to be engaged owners together, and to make decisions based on a common shared purpose. Engaged ownership is a choice that must affirmatively be made by each individual owner—an owner cannot be an engaged owner against her will, or consider himself engaged but just come along for the ride.

Third, this discussion of engaged ownership also presumes that there is more than one owner, and that most or all of the owners are related to each other. That is not because the issues discussed aren't relevant to an individual controlling owner, or to a group of unrelated owners of a private business. Dealing with ownership decisions—separate from family decisions and business decisions—can be a challenge even when just one person owns and controls a business, because whereas management focuses on the business, ownership decision-making requires a broader focus on core capital.

This discussion of engaged ownership focuses primarily on groups of owners because the dynamics of the family group make engagement that much more difficult for the owners to achieve. Within the group will be individuals with differing experience, perspective, skills, and personalities. They may be of different ages and from different branches or generations of the family. The group may include individuals who have roles beyond ownership, who serve as directors and/or members of the management team, for example. There may be one or more trustees, if all or part of the ownership is held in trust. One owner or a bloc may hold a controlling interest while others hold minority interests. The shares may be capitalized as voting and nonvoting, with the result that some owners may have different types and degrees of control over business decision making. All these differences can thwart individual efforts to develop consensus and become engaged owners. Where a diverse group owns a business, it can seem easier—and perhaps, safer—to delegate ownership decision making to one or two individuals than to undertake the work of becoming engaged owners.

Because of the challenges of overcoming such diversity, many advisors have argued that families should avoid group ownership. They recommend concentrating ownership and control in the hands of those who run the business. Certainly, many successful multigenerational family businesses have followed this strategy (sometimes referred to as "pruning the tree"). But those families that prefer to remain in business together can take heart; for those willing to put in the effort, engaged ownership offers the potential for a successful and sustainable path forward. And furthermore, engaged ownership by a group harnesses more of the human capital of the family in service of the business and the core capital. Non-managing owners bring valuable outside experience—employment in other industries, board service, life knowledge, academic training—to their work as owners, which can deepen and broaden the vision for the future of the business and the core capital.

Non-managing owners bring valuable outside experience—employment in other industries, board service, life knowledge, academic training—to their work as owners, which can deepen and broaden the vision for the future of the business and the core capital.

Impediments to Engaged Ownership

One might reasonably ask at this point, "Why aren't all family owners engaged?" There are any number of reasons why owners may not become involved in the decision making around the future of the business. Surprisingly few have anything to do with the owners themselves.

- Publicly held corporations have an outsized influence on the legal and organizational structures used by privately held corporations. As a result, there is a bias toward management-centric public company governance based on the fundamental assumption that shareholders seek financial returns.
- Conventional wisdom counsels that concentrating power in management is the only way to avoid infighting among owners with different objectives. Controlling owners may define succession planning narrowly as a search for a successor controlling owner. As a result, families that have the aptitude for and interest in engaged ownership may not consider it as an option, or plan or prepare themselves for engagement.
- Business-centric thinking around succession planning—defining the problem as finding a suitable successor CEO—leads to plans that focus on continuing the business rather than sustaining core capital. Societal policies such as primogeniture have reinforced the bias toward thinking of succession planning as primarily a task of naming a successor CEO and preserving the business. In such an environment, thinking broadly about core capital and weighing options that might redeploy capital away from the business to new ventures may seem heretical.
- Inherited ownership is often denigrated ("trust fund baby," "born with a silver spoon"). Inheritors who don't work in the business may be told, "You didn't earn this," or "You were given this, so don't complain," and so are discouraged from engagement. In such a business system, financial capital invested in the business may be seen as belonging to the business, not the owners.
- Owners who take over from a strong and successful founder may fear that they will be unable to match the founder's success. For these inheritors, ownership may seem more like a yoke than an opportunity.

The Rise of the Public Company Model of Governance

The problem is, the public corporation model, designed to bring together financial investors and managers in need of capital, with the help of a market that would provide an exit for unhappy investors, doesn't really fit owners who have received their shares through inheritance or estate planning transactions.

The rise of the public company model of corporate governance has had an outsized and sometimes pernicious effect on decision making in family businesses. In the earliest business transactions, there were no corporations or partnerships—people made products or provided services to each other in exchange for other products or services in a simple two-way barter economy. As people came together and local economies grew, currencies came about, which facilitated trade among multiple people simultaneously, simplifying transactions and creating a market for goods and services. As goods and services became more varied and sophisticated, and as economies of scale grew, businesses became more capital intensive.

Along with the need for capital came investors, a separate class of market participants who provided capital to producers in exchange for a financial return. Investors were understandably wary of investing in businesses without some ability to oversee the producers and make sure that capital would be put to the use intended, and not wasted or stolen, and so economies developed rules and systems—eventually encoded into law—that defined the relationships between the parties. But the need of the investors to oversee directly those who used their capital still limited the potential size of the business.

Arguably the most game-changing invention in the history of business was the creation of the corporation. The corporate form offered limited liability to investors along with a Board of Directors with the legal obligation oversee the business on their behalf. Whereas an investor in a joint venture or general partnership had unlimited liability and might stand to lose more money than he or she put in if things went very wrong, an investor in a corporation risked only his or her investment. Suddenly, corporate shareholders could enjoy an assymetric risk/return profile: If the business was successful, they could multiply their investment many times over; if it failed miserably, they could lose no more than their initial investment. The creation of what would be the modern-day corporation and the capping of investment risk enabled producers to recruit investors and their financial capital on an entirely new scale—under the new structure, investors enjoyed sufficient protections that they were willing to make more significant investments and accept less direct oversight. Public companies grew rapidly in many industries, with large groups of unrelated investors subscribing to new stock offerings in a wide range of businesses, and with public stock exchanges permitting investors to buy, sell, and trade shares at will.

Over time, the corporation became the most common form of business entity. Variations abounded—limited partnerships, limited liability companies—but all were built on the concept of treating investors separately from producers, and protecting their financial investments by limiting their financial risk. As a result, the public corporation governance is built on the notion that investors have purely a financial interest, and that they need to be protected from management, who might otherwise misuse the capital provided by the investors. Large and ever-expanding bodies of corporate law have spelled out the fiduciary duty of directors, whose job it is to oversee the business and management, in an ongoing attempt to balance the need to provide investors with a degree of protection while leaving management with sufficient leeway to make business decisions that will generate profit. Public company governance seeks to give unrelated investors reasonable transparency regarding the financial performance of the business, along with a robust market so that investors can buy and sell shares at will.

With a long and successful track record of promoting economic growth, and a robust and long-established body of legal rules and precedent, the corporation has become the leading structure for business entities in the United States, as well as a prominent model for corporate entities globally. Many family businesses aspire to operate "like a public company" and adopt governance practices (such as creating boards of independent directors) that mirror those of public corporations. The problem is, the public corporation model, designed to bring together financial investors and managers in need of capital, with the help of a market that would provide an exit for unhappy investors, doesn't really fit owners who have received their shares through inheritance or estate planning transactions. These family owners haven't purchased their shares—they've inherited them. Most family businesses are privately held and there is no market for trading in the shares.

Furthermore, to the family that owns it, a family business is much more than an investment: It is the embodiment of an ancestor's dream, the place where the owners worked during the summers, the enterprise where their ancestors developed new products or technologies that radically changed markets, the source of the contributions the owners have made to civic and charitable organizations, the employer of citizens in their town. A family-owned business is a venture built from the vision, hard work, and gumption of a family over generations. Engaged owners redefine the role of the owner to reflect their broad interest in core capital, and the reality that, for them, ownership is far more than a financial interest.

PART II

Getting Organized

Owen Family—June 2, 2011

Michael Owen, Age 41, President of Owen Products, Ltd.

It was a complete shock when my father died. I was coming home from a sales convention when I got the call on my mobile phone. My dad had been so healthy, we all expected him to live into his nineties, at least. The memorial service was amazing—just about all our suppliers and customers came. He was so well liked, my dad. The success of Owen Products is a testament to him—he grew it from a small company that my grandfather started in 1948. Sixty-two years later, we're the biggest terra cotta pot manufacturer in the country, with the highest quality. That's a tough act to follow. Our customers depend on us, and we deliver. Sometimes I wonder if I'm really the guy to do this job, but then I think, my granddad and dad learned to do it, so I can, too.

The company means a lot to me. Knowing all that goes into making our pots, and everything we've sacrificed as a family to stay in this business, keeps me motivated. My grandmother gave her most prized possession, her grandmother's diamond ring, for this business. My grandfather sank every penny he earned back in the business and then rebuilt the plant after the kiln explosion in 1959. My dad opened Owen Products West and tripled the size of the business. So now it's my job to lead it forward. I think my sisters and brother feel the same way about our family and Owen Products. I'd like to see all our kids come to work here.

My wife, Jane, reminds me that as much as she loves her mother-in-law, she's not willing to make the same sacrifices my mom did. She knows I didn't get to see my dad that much, and she doesn't want our twins, Cate and Chloe, to grow up without their dad. She has told me in no uncertain terms that I need to expand the management team so that I won't be traveling between the two plants all the time. But how am I going to make sure that the place is running properly if I'm not there?

Martha Owen Jones, Age 40, Homemaker

My dad was an amazing guy. We didn't always get to see him—he traveled all the time—but we knew he loved us. He was very driven. I've tried to adopt my mom's attitude about the company; we all make contributions and sacrifices and it has a little bit of all of us in it.

I'm tied to Owen Products two ways now—by my shares, and by my husband Ryan's job running operations at Owen Products West. I used to work at the company, in sort of a sideways way working on the community fund, but I retired when Ryan and I had our son, Jameson, in 1998. My mom raised four kids while Dad was away all the time—I have no idea how she did it. Ryan is still at Owen Products because he always had a lot of respect for my dad. It's tougher for Ryan now that Charlie is gone. Mike doesn't have the same operations background and really depends on Ryan to keep Owen Products West running. I think Mike should give Ryan a major raise and a promotion, and I told him so last week.

I'd really like to see Jameson join the business after university. He's already talking about studying ceramic engineering. He wants to be just like his dad, granddad, and great-granddad.

Amanda Owen Cooper, Age 35, Attorney

This family business needs some professionalization! As a partner at a major firm here in the West, I have had the opportunity to work with a number of family-owned businesses, and I've learned that to succeed in the third generation you can't just keep doing the same things—you've got to get organized. If we're going to be successful, I'd like to see us put in place some of their practices: create a shareholders agreement, bring on more independent directors, reorganize the management team, restructure compensation and distributions. Sometimes I wonder why Ryan, who's married to my sister, Martha, and also runs our western facility, puts up with us. Martha told me that Ryan has been offered a great job by our biggest competitor, but Mike isn't paying any attention since he's focusing on some issue back East.

I'm on the board, but I don't know how much I can help. I've got my hands full here, between my job, raising our little boys, Eric and Pete, and now, on top of all that, being trustee of Alfred's trust. My family has always stood for taking care of each other, and the company has always been our safety net. As the company and the family get bigger, how are we going to be able to keep those promises to each other? Would it be better to sell the business and protect our capital, rather than keep risking it?

Christopher Owen, Age 34, Professor

I'm an associate professor at Eastern University, in the Applied Mathematics department. Last week, I was notified that my team has received a government grant to further our work in combustion synthesis. We are developing methods to create nanoscale catalysts through high-temperature combustion. My family looks at me like I'm from Mars sometimes, but it's an entirely logical progression. My grandfather and David Smith developed new techniques to fire clay, and I'm just using firing techniques for a different purpose.

With this grant, my team will be able to refine our combustion processes. There are infinite industrial applications for this technology. To realize the full possibilities is going to take all my time and effort.

My apologies for cutting this short—I am late for a meeting.

Owen Family—July 5, 2011

Martha Owen Jones

The four of us agreed that we should meet to hold a shareholders meeting, to talk about Owen Products. Together, we own the Company—the four of us each own 18.75 percent individually, and Amanda also owns 25 percent as trustee for Alfred's trust. When we realized that she legally owns 43.75 percent, we were worried that she would try to make all the decisions about the company. But she reminded us that as a trustee, she has a duty to make decisions for the trust's shares solely for Alfred's benefit, not her own, so in a way she is like two separate shareholders.

I agreed to be secretary for our shareholder group and to keep minutes of all of our meetings. I used to do this for our sorority, so my past practice comes in handy.

We made a chart showing our roles. Mike has all four roles: he is the president of the company, he is a director, he is an owner, and he is a family member. Amanda is in three: she is a director, owner, and family member (we put her in as owner twice to represent her

	Manager	Owner	Director	Family
Mike	X	x	x	x
Martha		x		x
Amanda		xx	x	x
Christopher		x		x

Figure II.1   Owen Family Roles (as of February 2010)

trusteeship). David and I are in two roles: we are owners and family members. That led us to ask, what about spouses? Mike reminded us that Dad and Granddad always talked about keeping ownership to bloodline family. I pointed out that Mom and Nanna Leah had been as critical to our success as Dad and Granddad. We decided that our definition of *family* would include spouses and children, and at Christopher's recommendation, we included significant others who have been with a family member for more than four years, to include Christopher's girlfriend, Amatya. Amanda wanted us to begin working on a shareholders agreement right away, but we decided to start slowly and figure out where we are headed with Owen Products before we tackle policies on who can be an owner of the company.

Our first formal task as owners is to approve the slate of directors, at the annual shareholders meeting. Mike was ready to keep the board as it is, but Amanda suggested that we add two more independent directors to the slate who would help us "professionalize." (That is her mantra, "Professionalize." Sometimes, the rest of us roll our eyes when she gets on her high horse, but she has a point, because owning Owen Products is a huge responsibility.) Mike got annoyed, because Dad always chose the board and now that he is president, he felt he should have the same powers. Amanda reminded him that ultimately the owners are responsible for appointing the board. Dad wore all the hats when he was alive—he owned 75 percent of the shares, ran the company, chaired the board, and was head of our family, so it wasn't always clear what role he was in when he made a decision. Anyway, all of us—even Mike—agreed that it would be good to add some strategic planning expertise and some combustion technology expertise to the board, and that one of the new directors should come from the East and one from the West, for balance. We talked for a while about candidates. Amanda is going to ask one of her neighbors, a third-generation owner of a successful ceramic tile manufacturing business, if he would be interested. Christopher, to our surprise, recommended a colleague from Eastern University's business school who specializes in strategic planning, who has been working with his team in the Applied Mathematics Department. Christopher is always surprising us, because he appears to be lost in the clouds and then he comes up with some really good ideas.

Toward the end of our meeting, Christopher suddenly said, "I think we need to decide our capital structure." We must have all looked more than a little puzzled, because he began talking about capital and investment opportunities and mezzanine financing, and about debt and equity. Apparently, he has been reading up on businesses and he has some ideas. I reminded everyone that we want to start with the question why we want to be shareholders together, because, except for a few years between Uncle Fred's retirement and his passing, Owen Products has never had owners who didn't work in the business. This is a completely new state of affairs and we need to go carefully and keep ourselves aligned as a group. Two things we want to keep in mind: we want to preserve our family, and we want to do the right thing for the business. Now we just need to figure out what "the right thing" actually means for us.

4

Family Business Roles and Relationships

Roles

Within a family enterprise, there are four distinct roles: Owners, Board, Managers/Employees, and Family. Some individuals will play more than one role; some may play all four. Be forewarned: the descriptions below may seem foreign to owner-managers who run their businesses, because the distinctions may seem unnecessarily specific, particularly the description of the independent board. The independent Board of Directors described in this section has become increasingly common as family businesses have borrowed governance practices from public companies, but certainly not all family enterprises have boards comprised of a majority of non-family industry specialists. We have used the independent board here, not to enter the debate over advisory versus fiduciary boards, or to recommend one form of board over the other. Independent directors can bring experience, expertise, connections, and perspective; they can also bring assumptions about the purpose and strategy of the business that don't align with the owners' shared purpose or vision for the core capital. We've highlighted the independent board here because it can create impediments to engaged ownership that a family/owner-driven board might not, by further distancing owners from active participation in decision making.

Owners

Owners hold the ultimate power in the enterprise system,
because only they have the ultimate power to form, sell, or
shutter the enterprise, and to reinvest core capital within
the business or redeploy it outside the business.

Owners are the legal owners of the enterprise. This ownership
interest means that they hold the ultimate power in the enterprise
system, because only they have the ultimate power to form, sell,
or shutter the enterprise, and to reinvest core capital within the
business or redeploy it outside the business. All decision-making
power thus flows from ownership; typically, the owners reserve
some decision-making powers (for example, electing directors) and
delegate other decision-making powers to the board (for example,
approving strategy), though as we'll see, there is considerable
room for creative delegation of powers. Engaged owners organize
themselves and their interactions with overseers, management/
employees, and family to ensure that decision making is informed,
timely, and appropriate for their vision for the deployment of their
core capital. Owners receive distributions based on their percentage
ownership, which represent a return on the core capital invested in
the business.

Board

The board's primary role is as the chief overseer of the
enterprise.

This is the group most commonly known as the Board of
Directors, though it may be known as the Managers' Committee
in an LLC or the Board of Trustees in a charitable foundation.
Generally, the board's primary role is as the chief overseer of the
enterprise. The owners typically delegate to the board the responsibility for setting/approving strategy for the enterprise, hiring
senior management, and monitoring performance. The board

meets regularly—typically, quarterly—with senior management to review and evaluate performance in light of the strategic plan, and to consider opportunities and potential threats to the enterprise.

Directors represent the owners and owe fiduciary duties to the owners and the enterprise. They must act with loyalty, avoiding even the appearance of conflict of interest, and with due care.

The board will typically include the chief executive of the business and one or more owners, as well as one or more independent directors. A strong board brings perspective, knowledge, and industry access to assist and support management. Independent directors typically have high-level management or board experience in the business sector in which the business operates, and so can provide useful influence and contacts. Particularly for a smaller family business operating in a major industry, having one or more independent directors with public company experience can provide insight into industry practice that they otherwise might not be able to access. The board can thus be a potent force for bringing greater professionalization as well as financial and operational discipline to a family business.

Board members may hold shares in the business and may also receive compensation for their efforts.

Managers and Employees

Management carries out the work of the business.

The board, in turn, hires the chief executive of the business and typically delegates day-to-day decision-making and operational responsibilities to management. Management and employees then operate the business in accordance with the strategic plan approved by the board. In essence, they are responsible for carrying out the work of the business. Management is responsible for assembling the team and resources needed to accomplish the plan and managing the process on a day-to-day basis. Because management is closest to the operations, managers typically have the deepest knowledge of business and market conditions as well as tactical issues and opportunities that may exist. Management and employees receive compensation, and sometimes shares, in exchange for their efforts.

Family

For a family business, the family itself is the source of the entrepreneurial spirit and values that lie at the core of business culture.

For a family business, the family itself is the source of the entrepreneurial spirit and values that lie at the core of business culture. Every family business is different because every family is different. Family members may play other roles—managers, directors, owners—but their relationship as family members is always at the center of their decision making. Families define their boundaries differently—some define family to include bloodline descendants only while other families are highly inclusive of in-laws, stepchildren, and sometimes even former in-laws who are now divorced from family members.

Different Perspectives

Core capital is finite. Each group—management, board, owners, family—will have its own focus and strongly held views about how core capital should be deployed.

Four groups—owners, board, management, family—will have four different points of view. Given the different roles that each group plays within the family business, and the reality that core capital is finite, each group—management, board, owners, family—will have its own focus and strongly held views about how the capital should be deployed. Here again, the descriptions may seem too narrowly drawn to the owner-manager who serves in multiple roles, but our purpose is to describe the central focus of each group. Keep in mind that any one individual might belong in more than one (or perhaps even all) of the groups.

Management

Management will be business focused and will tend toward deploying available core capital to strengthen the business activities of the business. Depending on how compensation and bonuses are structured, management may have an incentive to promote and pursue options that increase their individual involvement in the business and the financial rewards they can receive over the course of their careers. As a general rule, members of management will prefer to retain core capital within the business rather than distribute it, and will prefer to continue existing businesses rather than redeploy capital into different business areas that would not be included under their aegis. Management might ask:

- How much inventory do we need to build this quarter to prepare for the holiday rush, and how will that investment impact our cash flow?
- Our sales manager is retiring; should we recruit from the industry or promote from within?
- What tactics will be most likely to enable us to hit our sales budget? Our profit targets?

Board

The *board*, in their role as *overseers*, will also be business focused but will tend to bring a longer-term, more strategic viewpoint as befits their more periodic involvement. Independent board members will tend to be well-schooled in business financial metrics but may have had little prior experience with privately held businesses and so may lack perspective on the value of non-financial core capital and the needs and perspectives of family owners. The board will tend to push management to perform better and achieve greater results (primarily from a financial viewpoint). The board may be more open than management to looking at investing in new businesses but will not generally look beyond the existing industry or business sector of the business. The board will generally prefer to have core capital retained within the business rather than distributed out or redirected to other opportunities. The board might ask:

- What is our strategy for growing market share?
- Is building inventory the best use for available cash, or should we invest in new equipment to reduce manufacturing cycle time?
- What are the career timelines for all senior staff, and are we preparing the next generation of leaders?
- We have cash; have we evaluated acquisition targets?

Family

Family will be interested in the business in different ways. Time and availability are elements of human capital, and family members who aren't involved in the business may push to have the business take up less of the family's time together. Some family members may seek employment or business opportunities from the business. Family members who don't participate in the business may nonetheless derive social standing in the community from it; they may enjoy additional social capital, a greater reputation in the community, and increased social or even business opportunities because of their association with the business and so may push for decisions that enhance social capital and against those that they feel would harm it, such as closing a manufacturing facility in the community. Family members might ask:

- Why do we always talk about the business at the dinner table?
- Will my children be able to look to the business for career opportunities?
- The company just announced it is closing our local manufacturing facility; will this affect my friendships within the community?
- When will I inherit shares?

Owners

Owners will be deeply interested in the performance of the business but will also tend to look more broadly at issues of how core capital should be deployed. They will look for a long-term return on their core capital, but also will seek to have the business deploy core capital in ways that support the shared purpose (which may puzzle or even frustrate non-family management and board who have a narrower, financial focus). They may seek to harvest core capital from a successful business in order to nurture a new entrepreneurial effort (particularly, an effort being developed by a family member), a move that might be opposed by board and non-family management alike. They may devote considerable time and energy exposing family to the business in order to build engagement in the next generation, which may seem unnecessary and intrusive to non-family management. Because owners have a broader view of capital than do board or management, owners may be more inclined than board and management to oppose a choice that damages human or enterprise capital, even if their opposition may impair financial capital to some degree. Trustee owners will have a somewhat different focus: their fiduciary duties will require them to make ownership decisions based on the needs of the beneficiaries of the trust, which may conflict with other owners' vision for the future of the core capital. Owners might ask:

- How will the proposed business strategy impact our ability to pay dividends in the future?
- Might this new, edgy marketing campaign hurt our hard-earned reputation in this town?
- Should we measure our success by local employment, or by social responsibility, or by environmental impact, and not just profits?
- Should we be investing in products and services being developed by talented family members, to carry on our family's legacy of innovation, even if that means pulling money away from the business?

Roles Affect Perspective

The biggest challenge for individuals in a family business is to recognize which roles they play and how those roles affect their perspective regarding the business.

The biggest challenge for individuals in a family business is to recognize which roles they play and how those roles affect their perspective regarding the business. One of the biggest challenges to engaged ownership occurs when an individual plays multiple roles, because playing multiple roles increases the odds that discussions will take place and decisions may even be made in the wrong forum without the knowledge or participation of others who should properly be part of the decision-making process.

When owners, board, management, and family recognize their roles, they can more clearly articulate their own position and also see how others perceive an issue. This self-awareness helps to develop empathy and increase the likelihood that business issues will be considered and addressed more thoroughly.

Owen Family—September 6, 2011

Alison ("Ali") Owen

It has been eye-opening and heartening in equal measure to watch my children begin to take on the task of being owners. I had pushed Charlie to put the shares in a trust and appoint one person as trustee, to minimize the risk of a major disagreement that would destroy the family, but he opted to follow family tradition and give the children the shares. Then, when the board voted Mike as president, I assumed he would simply take charge and the other three would go back to their own lives and not pay much attention to the company. Clearly, I was not giving our children enough credit—they recognize that they are owners, that their name is on the door, and that they are ultimately responsible for how the company goes forward. In particular, Martha's leadership is a surprise to me—once she decided to stop working when Jameson was born, she didn't pay all that much attention to the business (other than to stand up for her husband, Ryan, when she felt her dad or her brother didn't give him enough credit for his contributions at Owen Products). Now, she is leading the owners, but quietly, without any fanfare, toward what seems from my vantage to be a more organized, thoughtful, consensus-based decision-making process. Amanda and David want to jump to the meaty technical questions about structuring and financing, and Michael mostly just wants quick approval for his plans, but Martha pulls them back to the biggest questions, saying gently that there is a lot at stake here and they have the responsibility to do the right thing.

I was thinking this morning about how different Charlie's decision-making process was. He had watched his father from the time he was born—John and Leah told me stories about how Charlie would follow his father around the plant whenever he could—and he quickly adopted John's style. Every decision of any importance came directly to Charlie. He delegated very little, which often frustrated his employees and slowed down progress. Being at the center of every decision also meant that Charlie needed to be everywhere at once, and he started the crazy travel back and forth between the Eastern and Western facilities every week. But Charlie, like his father, John, didn't see his management style as inefficient. He saw doing everything as his job—the only way to keep everything under control and on track. His formal training was in engineering, not business, and he was far more comfortable when he could measure and calculate things himself. His name was on the door and he was responsible. His Uncle Fred, who owned the other 25 percent of the shares (John awarded them to Fred when Fred joined the business and took over the finances), might have insisted on a bigger role, but Fred was so drained by the dual responsibilities of managing the company's finances and taking care of his son, Alfred, after his wife died that he happily delegated control to Charlie. And Charlie always saw Fred as a surrogate father figure after John died, so I think Fred managed to keep Charlie aware of his interests in an indirect way.

CHAPTER

5

The Legacy of the Past: Natural Governance, Family History, and Culture

Natural Governance

The natural governance system might be called "how we do things around here," and it is one of the hallmarks of family businesses.

It would be a mistake to think that a family business without a formal, written governance system has no governance. All the groups in the family business system—family, owners, board, management—aspire to a state of equilibrium. Everyone wants to be free to attend to his or her needs, wishes, interests, and responsibilities, whatever they may be, without stepping on others' toes. To keep this equilibrium, many family businesses from their first days evolve a form of "natural governance" that is largely based on assumptions, expectations, and understandings, rather than the tangible structures and policies of a formal decision-making system. This natural governance system might be called "how we do things around here," and it is one of the hallmarks of family businesses.

Natural governance is particularly apparent when a family business is run by a controlling owner: an owner who owns a majority of the voting power and who also manages the business. This is because the controlling owner is at the center of all decision making and occupies all the main roles in the business—owner, director, manager, family member. Those around him just know the types of behavior or actions that will meet with his approval or disapproval. Furthermore, there is often little or no formal decision-making structure in a business led by a controlling owner and few hurdles to jump to get from idea to decision. Natural governance can be invigorating when it works well; those involved in the business feel in sync and enjoy working in an environment where decision making is quick and informal, and where there is little bureaucracy. For any business that is growing quickly and achieving success in a competitive market, natural governance can be a source of strategic advantage vis-a-vis organizations with more formal, structured decision making. This sense of being "in the zone," decision-wise, is part of the allure of startups and "fast" companies.

Sometimes, family businesses will have formal governance systems (bylaws, rules and regulations, policies) that are consciously ignored. This tends to happen when the governance system was created in a vacuum and not designed, adopted, and practiced by those within the system. Formal governance systems tend to be overlooked or overridden when they don't fit the organization's existing way of doing things or when they are imposed by one group without buy-in or participation from the other groups.

Natural governance can be very adaptable and resilient, but there often will come a time when "the way we do things around here" won't generate the answers and decisions needed to move the business forward. As complexity increases within the business and within the groups that make up family, owners, board, and management, there may come a time when the business participants need more formal processes and rules and greater clarity around roles and responsibilities to enable the participants to make effective decisions on a timely basis. This may happen when the business gets large enough that it needs a management team, or begins to operate in multiple locations (especially when those locations are at a distance from each other, whether in terms of geography, culture, or activity), or enters an industry with significant regulatory or compliance requirements. It can happen as the ownership group expands, perhaps as the controlling owner develops an estate plan that divides his ownership among his children.

Two particular changes are especially likely to tip natural governance systems into chaotic disorganization: management succession and ownership succession, especially when they occur simultaneously and unexpectedly. This is because the person around whom the controlling owner system was built, and whose patterns of decision making formed the core of the natural governance system, is suddenly absent and unable to reinforce prior decision making or create new precedents. When natural governance fails following unexpected succession, confusion spreads throughout the system and there may be attempts by an individual (usually, a family member in management) to step into the controlling owner role and reassert the natural governance system that existed under the controlling owner. Sometimes, such efforts are successful, and natural governance returns to a state of equilibrium. Sometimes, however, those within the system (management, family members, board, owners) reject the newcomer as the source of control and scramble to maximize their own power.

These are difficult moments for any business, because the business and its core capital will be at risk if the decision-making system flounders and a battle for control of the business is ignited. In such situations, refocusing around developing greater engagement among the ownership group and between owners, board, management, and family through a clear, transparent process of governance design that is accepted by all will help create a more effective base for decision making going forward.

Owen Family—October 4, 2011

Alison ("Ali") Owen

Ten months ago, Charlie died. We are all learning to manage without him but finding different ways to cope.

Mike is facing a quandary right now, though I'm not sure that he can see it clearly. His duty as president of the company, and his desire to be a good husband and father to twins, are in conflict. He is finding that his father's shoes and his wife's anger are both very uncomfortable, and I can see that he is worrying that he might let both the business and his family down. Perhaps, in a way, it is my doing that he finds himself at this crossroads, because I chose to honor the obligation Charlie felt to his parents and the business and so I picked up most of his responsibility for our children. It was a different era back in the 1970s, certainly, but I made the choice willingly in spite of having excellent career prospects of my own. I think that my mother-in-law Leah's example of giving up her grandmother's diamond ring to help fund the startup inspired me to make a gift to the business that would be a symbol of my own commitment.

Now, I am not so sure I would give everything for the business, and I am going to do what I can to let Mike know that he is not obligated to make the choice his father made. I also think that making the choice to manage differently, and to think about the business differently, might help his siblings and the business. It was never really possible for one person to manage the business by himself. Charlie just followed the path his father set, and he assumed it was the right path. All of us around him could see that the addition of the Western facility was both a great business idea and an impossible management task for one inclined to do it all himself. But Charlie needed to prove that he, like his father, could create an entirely new business. The problem is, the question wasn't whether he could do it; the real question was whether the investment was worth it. Mike will need to make his own choice, but I want him to make it with his eyes wide open, weighing the options and the cost.

The Enterprise as Family Member

A family business, created from the sweat of the founder and all the core capital that could be mustered over many years, often comes to be seen not just as a person but sometimes as the most-favored member of the family.

A family business, created from the sweat of the founder and all the core capital that could be mustered over many years, often comes to be seen not just as a person but sometimes as the most-favored member of the family. The business itself—its activities, customers, employees, premises, equipment, technology, brands—becomes the primary focus of family discussion, attention, and concern. Thus, the business may, like the prodigal son, become the recipient of inordinate amounts of time, attention, love, and resource.

For a family member who suddenly finds himself an owner of the family business, generally as the result of an estate planning transfer, the fact that the business is treated as a favored member of the family may make engagement more difficult to imagine and achieve. Children who have grown up around a business that has been treated as a favored family member will tend either to carry on that practice, or to recoil from the ownership role. This is because a business that was viewed by its founder as a special child comes to be seen by a child or grandchild who comes to own shares as an august and powerful personage, for good or for ill. The challenge for engaged ownership is that what begins as a learned attitude of respect can become a paralyzing fear of offending, with the result that the new shareholder is reluctant to take any action that might create disruption or hurt the business in any way.

But can respect be carried too far? The ugly truth is that well-managed businesses fail every day; markets evolve, governmental regulations are voted in and out, products go out of fashion, science and technology advance. A business that fails will take much of the core capital with it. Owners who take seriously their role in sustaining core capital will recognize that that role must include developing an ongoing conversation with board and family about how the core capital is being deployed, what risks and opportunities exist, and whether capital should be redeployed in other ways, even if that might mean downsizing the existing business or exiting it altogether. Owners who view the business as an august senior member of the family are less likely to ask the tough questions that engaged owners need to ask. This problem can be especially difficult when the business is performing poorly; if the business is considered a family member, it may receive life support in the form of major infusions of additional financial capital rather than the tough, thoughtful, swift, and measured action that may be needed to sustain the core capital.

Owen Family—October 4, 2011

Martha Owen Jones

It has been 10 months since Dad's death and all of us siblings, our husbands, wives, and children spent the day with Mom today. She is coping, though she seems lonely sometimes. Having the five grandchildren all together was fun. My son, Jameson, who just turned 13, got to spend some time with Mike and Jane's twin girls, who are 17 and applying to university this year. The three of them played with Amanda's sons, who are 6 and 4. It took a lot to get Christopher to come. He kept saying he had too much work, and too much travel, and his girlfriend Amatya had to teach, but he finally came.

Mom went off on a walk with the grandchildren after dinner, and we kids were hanging out in the living room of the old house drinking what was left of the wine. Christopher had enough to relax a little for once and explain his work in combustion synthesis to us. Amanda asked a lot of technical and legal questions, the way she always does, and Mike began asking him whether there were any applications of the technology that might be useful to Owen Products. Christopher said that our plant equipment was essentially prehistoric, but there were many applications of his technology that could ultimately change the way commercial greenhouses would operate, and that we should reconsider our long-term capital investment strategy.

Mike started to respond with our grandfather's mantra, "People will always want potted plants, and terra cotta is the best possible pot for growing them," when Amanda's husband, Paul, began to laugh. He has known Amanda—all of us, in fact—since we were kids, and he still remembers John. "You know, there are all these sayings you guys inherited along with the business: 'People will always want potted plants,' 'Do whatever it takes,' 'Keep the shares in the family.' Do you ever stop and think about these?"

We sort of looked at him for a moment, and then Mike said, "Always reinvest your cash flow." Amanda laughed and added, "Trust family first." My husband, Ryan, looked thoughtful and said, "Owens manage Owen Products." Mike's wife Jane nodded, and added, "Only distribute if you can't think of any other use for the cash."

The conversation continued in that vein for a while, and then got a little bit goofy as we thought about our dad and drank some more wine. But I can't help thinking about Paul's question. Maybe we need to reconsider some of the "rules" that have been handed down to us.

Culture, Attitudes, and Assumptions

Family businesses have especially strong and unique cultures, particularly those that were founder driven and founder funded for a substantial period of time.

All organizations have a culture, a collection of norms and practices, a distinct way of thinking about and expressing what they do. The culture of an organization is a complex product of the environment, the backgrounds, values, and attitudes of its founders and participants and their reactions and solutions to the challenges that they have grappled with over time. Edgar Schein[1] defines the culture of an organization as a pattern of shared basic assumptions learned by a group as it solved its problems—what works, and what doesn't.

Those assumptions become integral to the culture of the organization—how we do things around here—and part of the way that the group defines itself, in essence, its personality. Natural governance can thus be seen as part of the unique culture of a family business. Particularly to latecomers, culture is invisible, but highly pervasive and very like the oxygen in the atmosphere—hard to see, but always there.

Family businesses have especially strong and unique cultures, particularly those that were founder driven and founder funded for a substantial period of time. This is because one person has been at the center of decision making and control for decades, and that person's solutions to challenges—the way he defined the challenge and the resources he drew on to solve it, the tactics he used to rally others to the cause—become encoded in the culture. People around the founder—senior staff, employees, and outsiders including customers, suppliers, bankers, accountants, lawyers—all come to understand the founder's particular way of doing things and learn as best they can to operate successfully within the founder's orbit. (It should come as little surprise that founders who are highly charismatic or quick-tempered tend to produce very distinct cultures as those around them learn to accommodate their unique and possibly explosive decision-making style.)

Family businesses are also unique from a cultural standpoint, because the founder's attitudes and assumptions tend to shape the culture of the family as well as the business. As a result, children absorb many of those attitudes and assumptions from an early age. Most of these attitudes revolve around the importance of the business and the primacy of management in decision making. Consider a founder-run business that struggled to survive through a major recession: cash was tight, banks pulled credit lines and refused to lend, customers paid late or not at all, and management was forced to cut payroll. Survival depended on eliminating dividends, saving money wherever possible, and reinvesting every penny of cash flow. Possibly, family members contributed or loaned cash to the business to sustain operations. For the business that struggled through this difficult time but ultimately succeeded, the lessons "we tighten our belts" and "cash is king" would become embedded in the culture. But not only would the culture of the business come to reflect these new values; so would the culture of the family. Belt tightening and thrift would become core values of the family, reinforced through dinner table discussion and family policies.

"We tighten our belts" makes good business sense—at the right time. Aversion to debt or spending may stunt the business's growth in better times and hamper the growth of core capital. The challenge of cultural change that follows a traumatic period such as a deep recession or rapid and disruptive market change is that it may emphasize and promote attitudes and behaviors that don't suit all circumstances and environments.

Another common but less obvious attitude is "earn to own." In a society that reveres self-made entrepreneurs and looks askance at inherited wealth, a founding owner may impress upon his children the value of self-reliance and the importance of earning one's own way in the world. He may even create policies that award shares to those children that come to work in the business. If that founding owner then at some point in the future gives his shares in the business in equal shares to his adult children (perhaps through a sophisticated planning transaction that saves taxes and thereby preserves financial and business capital for the future), the owner might be well-pleased by the success of his planning. The adult children, however, may be at a loss; they have just received the very thing that their father worked hardest to create without having to do anything in return. The conflicting messages may become even more difficult to decipher if they are also told, "You were given your shares, you didn't earn them. Business decisions aren't yours to make." Such messages thwart engagement and may leave recipients both anxious and passive.

Difficult Conversations

> But however highly revered a business is by the family, owners, board, and management, the uncomfortable reality is that circumstances change and well-regarded, well-managed businesses fail every day.

Family businesses develop existences of their own, becoming living systems. In some family-business cultures it can be taboo for those who don't run the business to request money from it—such a request might be seen as unfair to the business or perhaps as a violation of the "earn to own" attitude. In other businesses, it can be taboo to discuss shrinking or exiting a business activity that has been conducted by the family over generations—such an action would be akin to ending the life of a family member. But however highly revered a business is by the family, owners, board, and management, the uncomfortable reality is that circumstances change and well-regarded, well-managed businesses fail every day. No business, no matter how revered, can be assured of permanent survival. And when a business fails, much of its financial, human, and enterprise capital is lost forever. As difficult as it may be for owners to stand up to family, management, and board to question whether it makes sense to continue in a business activity that has been part of a family's legacy for generations, it is important for engaged owners to look squarely at whether core capital is being deployed optimally and to engage the board and senior management on such questions. This ability—to come together with board and family to talk about business choices openly even when doing so may be taboo—is a hallmark of engaged ownership.

Endnote

1. Edgar Schein, *Organizational Culture and Leadership* (John Wiley & Sons, 2010).

Owen Family—January 28, 2012

Martha Owen Jones

At the suggestion of one of our new board members, the family busi-ness owner, we shareholders decided to hold a two-day retreat to discuss our core capital and articulate our shared purpose and vision for the future of Owen Products, Ltd. It was nearly impossible to get the four of us together, but the board has asked us to explain our vision before they undertake their strategic planning process for the coming fiscal year. We brought in a facilitator recommended by our other new board member, the business school professor. I'm glad we did it, because it turns out that we're not necessarily as aligned as we thought we were about the future of the company, and the facilitator kept us from interrupting each other and kept tensions from spilling over into arguments.

We learned a lot about the business and each other in this session. Before we even got started, Mike told us that he just wasn't sure he wanted the job of president. That caused us all to panic a bit and to try to solve the problem right then and there. Then Christopher said he just didn't have time for any of this and needed to get back to his office. Amanda kept looking at her phone. The facilitator helped us calm down, hold our ideas and complaints, and focus on the agenda. We had all committed to these two days together; were we, as owners, committed to coming to consensus on the path ahead? Since we knew we couldn't solve Mike's problem or deal with the leadership question until we had determined our shared purpose and vision for Owen Products, we agreed to stick with the plan for the retreat.

Starting with the core capital helped us get focused. We realized that we have all kinds of capital in many forms. Christopher was tense at first, but then he began to relax and participate a little, and his inputs were surprising—we had no idea he knew so much about ceramics manufacturing. He helped us recognize that our work at Owen Products is innovative even though we're in an old-line kind of industry. We also began to get excited thinking about all the processes and products our family has developed over decades and how we've helped create new businesses within Owen Products.

CORE CAPITAL OF OWEN PRODUCTS, LTD. AND THE OWEN FAMILY

Financial Capital:

- Annual sales—$30 million

- EBITDA—$2.5 million

- Debt—$3 million outstanding on $6 million line of credit at LIBOR + 2%, secured by inventory, real property, and equipment

- Capital investment budget—$2 million/year

We agreed to get an appraisal of the company to get an understanding of the value of our shares for estate planning purposes.

We agreed to engage an investment banker on a limited basis to get an understanding of the value of Owen Products compared with comparable companies.

Human Capital:

- Close-knit family, very well educated, loyal

- Ingenuity

- Owners interested in business and willing to be actively involved
- Excellent employer–employee relationships
- Reputation as an industry leader
- Reputation as a corporate good citizen in towns where plants are located
- Values: hard work, integrity, discipline, loyalty, safeguarding each other

Enterprise Capital:

- Extensive knowledge of ceramics manufacturing systems
- Deep knowledge of eastern and western regional clays
- Expertise in forming of complex shapes with ceramic materials
- Expertise in customizing firing environments to specific attributes of ceramic materials
- Expertise in doing business with numerous small greenhouse customers operating on very tight margins
- Expertise and custom logistics systems for doing business with major growers with stringent customer service requirement and timelines
- Process management expertise
- Legal expertise: water conservation regulations; greenhouse and grower regulations

Enumerating Core Capital

Core Capital

> Owners who recognize enterprise capital as part of their core capital will be less inclined to undervalue their businesses or overlook opportunities to invest in and generate a return from the savvy in their lineage.

There are potentially an infinite number of ways to define capital. While financial and human capital are widely recognized, enterprise capital may be less familiar. The ability to combine resources in ways that generate new value—enterprise capital—is a form of well-honed alchemy mastered by many business-owning families. Owners who recognize enterprise capital as part of their core capital will be less inclined to undervalue their businesses or overlook opportunities to invest in and generate a return from the savvy in their lineage.

As a refresher, this book looks at three types of core capital:

1. **Financial capital:** money and equivalents; the income and distributions from the business; the financial value of physical assets such as equipment, raw materials, inventories, and real estate.
2. **Human/social capital:** their individual and family relationships; their talents; drive, perseverance, grit and determination; their strongly held values and their entrepreneurial zeal;

the formal and informal education they've received and the experience and knowledge base they hold individually and as a group. (Social capital includes the family's relationships and connections; its influence, its values; the reservoir of goodwill and family members' good name within the family, the business, and the wider community.)

3. **Enterprise capital:** innovations in research, design, product, service, process; unique knowhow; combinations of capital unique to the family and its business that generate a return greater than what the separate elements would generate individually; the societal value of the product or service the business provides.

Financial Capital

A failing business will slowly destroy other forms of core capital as it consumes financial capital while a successful business will sustain and grow financial, human, and enterprise capital.

Financial capital is at the core of any business. A failing business—one that consumes financial capital rather than generating it—cannot endure. In developing their shared purpose and vision, owners may not put profitability first on their list of priorities, but profitability and positive cash flow will need to be achieved and sustained if the core capital in all its forms is to be sustained. That is because a failing business will slowly destroy other forms of core capital as it consumes financial capital while a successful business will sustain and grow financial and other forms of core capital.

Key questions for engaged owners around financial capital are:

- What is the business worth if it were to be sold? What is the business worth on a going-concern basis?
- How much free cash flow does it generate?
- Is the cash flow expected to be distributed to owners or reinvested?
- What are the longer-term prospects for the income stream from the business? Is this business expected to become more profitable, or less?

- How much capital reinvestment will be necessary to sustain the revenue stream over time?
- How leveraged is this business?
- How does the economic return to the owners compare with what would be generated if the business were sold and the financial capital deployed in a different business or invested in a securities portfolio?

The financial statements of the business will be the owners' starting point in determining what the business is worth and how much cash it generates. Owners who don't have a financial background should be forewarned that the demands of tax reporting and accounting methods often result in financials that satisfy the Financial Accounting Standards Board, the Internal Revenue Service, and other regulators but don't reliably indicate profitability as owners would seek to understand it. Furthermore, different types of businesses and different industries account differently. For example, manufacturing businesses that are building inventory for future sales may show a paper profit; they will also show negative cash flow. If the business will sell the inventory in the reasonable future (if the inventory is "good" inventory), then odds are good the investment will pay off, the profits will be realized, and cash will increase in the future. However, if the inventory isn't salable, then the cash invested in inventory was wasted and the profit shown on the financial statements is fictitious. Engaged owners who don't have sophisticated financial knowledge and understanding of how a particular business and industry make money will want to discuss the financials with the chief financial officer of the business and perhaps with other knowledgeable individuals to understand the financial statements, whether the business is profitable, and whether it is generating or using cash, and why.

Theoretically, the owners can determine one measure of financial capital from the balance sheet of the business by looking up shareholders equity on the balance sheet. However, in practice owners will need to look at financial capital through several different lenses in order to gain a full understanding of the financial capital of the business.

Asset Value

One way of valuing a business is by adding together the fair market value of the assets, then subtracting the liabilities. The balance sheet of the business can be a good place to begin looking at valuation, but further inquiry will be needed. That is because the balance sheet of the business generally shows assets at historic value, before depreciation. The actual value of assets (land, equipment, inventory, investments, intellectual property) is known as *fair market value* and is defined as the price a willing buyer would pay a willing seller for the asset. The challenge for owners is that the fair market value of an asset may vary (sometimes wildly) from the values shown on the financial statements, which generally reflect adjusted cost. Assets might be worth multiples or fractions of their cost depending on age, condition, location, or alternative use. Land that was purchased when it was cheap scrub farmland or an abandoned brownfields industrial site may now be located in a booming industrial park or urban area. Custom-designed and -built equipment or software was expensive to purchase and so will be shown at a high valuation, yet may be so specialized that no other business would find it useful, with the result that it would bring little or no value at resale. For businesses with substantial intangible assets such as goodwill, asset value will understate the value of the business. It is important for engaged owners to understand the major assets owned by the business, but their inquiry will need to be broader if they are to understand the financial core capital their ownership represents.

Going-Concern Value

Businesses are often worth more than their net asset value—sometimes, much more. A profitable business may generate net cash flow substantially in excess of the rate of return the assets would generate if sold and the proceeds reinvested in, say, a portfolio of public securities. Much of that going-concern value may be due to the enterprise capital of the business, such as goodwill, brand value, loyal customers, specialized knowledge or processes, or industry relationships. Going-concern value may also rise and fall with the fate of the industry the business is part of, and the state of the business cycle (a business may be worth more when the biggest players in the industry have cash and are looking to consolidate and/or expand sales by acquiring smaller players, and worth less during a recession, when those same industry leaders are cash-strapped and having difficulty raising or borrowing expansion capital). An appraiser or an investment banker familiar with the industry in which the business operates can help the owners understand what the business is worth on a going-concern basis.

Risk Profile

Once the owners understand the return profile of the business, they will want to consider risk. The business may generate strong net cash flow but be considerably riskier (or less risky) than alternative businesses the owners could invest in. Risk changes constantly: for example, the business cycle may lead banks to stop lending; the business's success may be based on a technological capability—or even a fashion craze—that abruptly becomes obsolete. A business that focuses on a single product or service is likely riskier than a diversified business in the same industry.

Leverage

Leverage is another risk factor that engaged owners will want to consider. Judicious borrowing can fuel growth, but too much borrowing can suck cash out of the business in the form of interest payments. When a business is significantly leveraged, the owners' equity may be imperiled in a downturn; if sales (and receivables) slow to the point that there is not enough cash to make scheduled interest and principal payments, the lender may foreclose on the loan, thereby putting the entire business at risk or forcing management to seek another (potentially more expensive) source of cash.

Return to Owners

Some family businesses make no distributions to owners. Management, the board, and owners may have agreed to reinvest all free cash flow and net profits back into the business. But sometimes, the decision not to pay dividends may not be rooted in the need to fund capital investments. Sometimes, the practice of not paying distributions may have begun when accountants pointed out that compensation, which is deductible for income tax purposes, is a more tax-effective way to pull money out of the business than distributions. Whatever the reason for not paying dividends, the practice may well become a policy over time: "We don't make distributions from this business." When the founding owner passes on the shares, the new owners may find that the "no dividends" policy is assumed to be still valid in spite of the change of circumstances.

This policy can create unequal outcomes for managing owners versus non-managing owners, to the extent that the compensation paid to the managing owner exceeds market rates. Owners of such a business own a non-performing asset (from their perspective); they may find engagement more difficult to achieve if there is no reasonable expectation of a return on their shares.

Relative Return

What return would the financial capital generate if it were invested in a different business or in a portfolio of securities? This is not a simple exercise: Along with evaluating the positive returns other investments might offer, the owners must consider the risks, the taxes, and the transaction costs of dismantling an existing business, not to mention the time spent, the learning curve, and the disruption that would be caused by a radical change in how the financial capital is invested.

To some founders and their families, a business is akin to an epic quest: an all-consuming effort to harness an idea and bring an innovative product or service to customers.

To some founders and their families, a business is akin to an epic quest: an all-consuming effort to harness an idea and bring an innovative product or service to customers. This quest is often not about profit per se; founders are willing to take on substantial risk and hardship to prove out their vision, and they create a strong value within their families regarding the importance of the business. Indeed, the business may have created and nurtured substantial human capital and enterprise capital that is highly valued by the family owners and that would be lost if the business were to be shuttered. However, if the business cannot reasonably be expected to create sufficient financial returns to sustain the human capital and business capital over the long haul, it will ultimately consume financial capital. The owners—the ultimate holders of the equity—have the ultimate power and the responsibility to decide whether the business should continue, whether it should change its overall strategy, or whether an alternative deployment of the capital would help the owners and their family achieve their shared purpose. The owners may choose nonetheless to continue a business that performs less well than the alternatives for any number of reasons, but they will want to recognize and acknowledge the choice they are making.

But before engaged owners even consider making a decision about the future of the business, they will want to evaluate their other forms of capital: human capital and enterprise capital.

Human Capital

Human capital is the sum total of the family's individual and collective human potential.

Human capital is the sum total of the family's individual and collective human potential. It reflects family members' aptitudes, abilities, and talents; their drive, perseverance, grit and determination; their strongly held values; and their entrepreneurial zeal. Human capital reflects the formal and informal education family members have absorbed and the experience and knowledge base they hold individually and as a group. It is the values the family stands for: the actions concerning which they will say, without question, "We always" or "We never." Human capital includes social capital: the family's relationships and connections; its influence and its values; the reservoir of goodwill and family members' good name within the family, the business, and the wider community.

Human capital includes the owners and the members of the owners' family, of course, but it also includes those who bring their individual human capital to the business: employees, board, advisors, as well as other stakeholders such as suppliers, customers, and even competitors. Human capital is the reason other forms of capital have value: without human contributions of purpose, vision, and drive, financial capital sits idle.

The greater the human capital in the business and in the industry and market in which it operates, the more likely it is that financial and enterprise capital will achieve above-average returns. Human capital is necessary to find opportunity, to create the plan to capture it, and to deploy resources—financial and enterprise capital—to execute the plan. If human capital is lacking, if there isn't sufficient will, knowledge, and experience to carry out this process, the plan may not succeed.

Human capital is unique because it is embodied in human beings, who have a finite lifespan. As a result, human capital that isn't passed on via education, mentoring, documenting processes and ideas may simply disappear. Furthermore, individuals who don't find a place in the business for their talents, skills, and interests may choose to leave, taking their human capital with them.

For these reasons, family business owners who reflect on the relative importance of the different types of core capital may well conclude that human capital is the most important of the three types of capital, because it is the engine from which the other types of capital are powered. Furthermore, human capital, if nurtured, can regenerate financial and business capital. Families and family businesses that focus on investing in human capital and building their collective pool of human capital in the family as well as the business may be best positioned for long-term success because they are focused on keeping the engine running. Investments in human capital may include education, mentoring, coaching, team-building, and attention to creating and sustaining a culture that helps individuals maximize their contributions.

Business-owning families are apt to value business management skills and talents within the family above all. This is in large part because business succession planning has so often been framed as a task focused on finding a successor from the next generation who can run the business. Once a capable manager has been identified, everyone sighs with relief and goes back to their individual interests; the business is safe; the business will continue. But this business-first, management-first attitude means that not enough thought may be given to what other skills and talents might be needed in other roles within the family-business system, and how the system might usefully deploy more of the human capital available to it. For example, who has the emotional intelligence needed to serve as trustee? Who has the broader worldview needed to be an effective director? Who has an entrepreneurial mindset and the drive to create a completely new business? Who has the patience and focus to coach and mentor young professionals or to systematize and operationalize the brilliant but erratic ideas of the founder? Owners who invest in building human capital within the business and the family, who learn to spot skills and talents, nurture them, and put them to best and highest use, will create a more effective pathway to long-term success.

Enterprise Capital

Enterprise capital is the end result of human capital that has been coupled with financial capital to accomplish a specific endeavor.

Enterprise capital is all the unique knowhow embodied within the business; it is the array of one-of-a-kind combinations of capital unique to the family and its business that generate a return greater than what the separate elements would generate individually. Enterprise capital is the end result of human capital that has been coupled with financial capital to accomplish a specific endeavor: a machine, a system, an algorithm or a technique that enables a product to be made or a service to be delivered more quickly, artfully, efficiently, safely, economically, ergonomically—in short, better—than the competition could do it. Enterprise capital is what enables a business to generate above-average returns. To begin seeing enterprise capital, ask: What does the business do particularly well, and what are the combinations of human and financial capital that enable us to do it?

Enterprise capital is not necessarily fixed or permanent—it can be appropriated, copied, or imitated by competitors, or made redundant by changes in the market or technology—but the possibility of creating new and valuable enterprise capital is what drives entrepreneurial activity in families and businesses. The most successful businesses are not satisfied with the status quo and constantly create new enterprise capital.

Enterprise capital creates advantages and opportunities: a family with knowhow can leverage it in the existing business (by using it to expand into new products, services, or markets) or in entirely new businesses. For example, at a basic level, the existing financial infrastructure of a business—experienced and highly trained staff equipped with sophisticated computer systems and established financial reporting practices—represents enterprise capital that can be used to support a new business venture the family might wish to start. Having access to this enterprise capital offers substantial advantages to the new venture's leaders, because they can focus on the startup without also having to simultaneously develop administrative infrastructure. Similarly, the new venture might also be able to leverage existing enterprise capital in the form of technical knowhow, borrowing systems developed for one product or service and tweaking them in some way that enables them to be used in the new venture.

Enterprise capital is at the center of family business success, but it also creates opportunities outside the business. Access to knowhow and systems and connections with suppliers, customers, clients, and advisors can create opportunities for family members to learn about business generally and to begin developing new enterprise capital. Working in a family business at any level can be a first step toward running the company, certainly, but it can also help a family member develop a successful career outside the family business. Those who have worked in the business but choose to focus their careers elsewhere will nonetheless have greater insight into the business when it comes to participating in the family-business system in other roles: engaged owner, trustee, beneficiary, director, or advisor. Those who had firsthand experience with the enterprise capital but who are now employed elsewhere may identify new opportunities that are invisible to others.

Owners who are considering whether to sell a business will want to make sure that they think about the unique combinations of human, financial, and enterprise capital of their business that would disappear with the sale. With a potential sale comes the siren call of financial capital: the promise of liquidity and relief from the day-to-day fears and frustrations that come with owning and operating a business. Liquid capital is indeed lower risk than business capital; it can be invested immediately in securities that will generate a financial return without the financial rollercoaster ride that business ownership can entail. But financial capital will not achieve the returns that an operating business can achieve until it is combined again with human capital to create new enterprise capital. It is not surprising that some owners who sell businesses gravitate to venture capital, angel investing, and direct investing, preferring the more familiar (perhaps exhilarating) ride of an investment in a startup company to the security of a blue-chip stock or bond. Those that create new enterprise capital by bringing their own expertise to the selection of the investment, or perhaps by joining the Board of Directors or otherwise providing strategic guidance to the startup, will often find greater success, measured in terms of personal satisfaction as well as financial return. Those families who sell a business and passively invest the proceeds may achieve a measure of financial security, but they may also limit family members' exposure and access to enterprise capital and the opportunities it can generate, with the result that entrepreneurial efforts go unsupported and little new enterprise capital is created.

Engaged owners will recognize that enterprise capital, like financial and human capital, can be deployed in activities far beyond the existing business. Engaged owners can be particularly important in helping the family-business system recognize enterprise capital, identify new opportunities for deploying it beyond the existing business, and foster new combinations of human and financial capital that can create entirely new enterprise capital. Recognizing enterprise capital as part of the owners' and family's opportunity set and consciously seeking to deploy it within and beyond the existing business is one important way that engaged owners can multiply the financial, human, and enterprise capital that their ownership represents.

How to Enumerate Core Capital

Enumerating core capital is an exercise of thinking about all that has been invested in the business and the family over time—all the assets, in all forms, that make up their legacy and their future opportunity set.

Enumerating core capital is an exercise of thinking about all that has been invested in the business and the family over time—all the assets, in all forms, that make up their legacy and their future opportunity set. Financial institutions and media will focus on financial capital, but the owners will want to dig deeper. The group may begin the exercise by asking itself: What has been invested in this family and this business over generations? It may also be helpful to ask:

- What have been the most successful investments of capital?
- What does this business do better than its competition?
- Have there been occasions where capital has been lost or even wasted?

It can be helpful to look at core capital from different vantage points:

- *What is our financial capital?* What is this business worth on a going-concern basis? What are its assets worth? What would our shares be worth after tax if we were to sell them?

- *What is the human capital of the family?* What is the unique human capital within the business? Within our family? What are our values? What is our reputation in the community? What are the lessons this business has taught us? Are we using all the human capital available to us?
- *What is the enterprise capital of this business?* What do we do exceptionally well and what are the specific processes/equipment/ systems/capabilities that enable us to do those things? How else might we use this capital?

One member volunteers as scribe. Using a flipchart, the group sets up three separate pages, one for each of the types of core capital. Then, one by one, each member of the group offers up a specific example of a type of capital.

It is easiest to go around the group in a set order, which avoids the problem of one member of the group dominating the discussion. To maximize the benefit of the exercise, the group must avoid the temptation to judge, criticize, improve, rank, or otherwise evaluate the vision elements during this first pass. The goal is simply to get all the possible elements of the vision out on paper. There is no right or wrong in this exercise.

Once the types of capital have been enumerated, ask:

- Are we using our core capital effectively?
- What other opportunities exist where we might deploy capital?
- What other opportunities exist where our human and financial capital might be combined to create new enterprise capital?

Enumerating core capital is an important place to start the exercise of getting organized because it reminds the owners exactly what is at stake. Owners who spend time grappling with the concept of core capital will recognize that while financial capital is owned by individuals (at least in a legal sense), human capital is owned collectively. Financial capital invested by itself will generate a financial return; financial capital coupled with human capital will generate enterprise capital, which has the opportunity to achieve above-average returns.

Owen Family—January 28, 2012

Martha Owen Jones

Mike was particularly active in our discussion about shared purpose. Having been part of management of Owen Products for years, he is incredibly familiar with the business and what goes on there. He has a special appreciation for our employees, and how important Owen Products is to the communities where we operate.

As we were working on the shared purpose around ownership of the business, I began thinking about the fact that our ownership goes beyond the business; part of our desire to work together as owners is to make sure we use the capital for the future of our family, whether we do that in the business or not. Our dad and granddad always focused on Owen Products, but our discussion today got a lot more interesting when we started thinking about the wider purpose of our core capital. We talked about Amanda's responsibilities to Alfred, who depends on the shares in his trust to fund his care, and our responsibilities to our own children. We have a lot more respect for Amanda's responsibilities as trustee now, and what that means for the business. Then we talked about ways we might use our capital for the family's benefit—not necessarily by spending it on things, but by investing it in opportunities created by our family. That made us wonder: How can we help Christopher be successful? At first, Mike was inclined to challenge any notion that we might harvest profits from Owen Products to help fund other businesses, but when Amanda pointed out that his twin daughters, Cate and Chloe, both of whom are interested in medicine, not the clay pot industry, might want to use family capital to invest in their careers, Mike softened up a bit.

DRAFT: SHARED PURPOSE OF THE OWNERS OF OWEN PRODUCTS, LTD.

We want to be owners in this business together because:

- We have a deep respect for the effort, commitment, and sacrifice of our parents and grandparents to build this business and we want to continue their work.

- We want to build on our collective knowledge of terra cotta production techniques and ceramic firing techniques.

- We are a major employer in the towns where our plants are located and we understand that our employees' livelihoods depend on our success.

- We encourage participation and leadership by Owen family members, taking into consideration the needs of our business.

I'm torn on this. My husband, Ryan, is completely focused on Owen Products, and Jameson wants to be just like his dad, his grand-dad, and his great-granddad and really understand the mysteries of what our clays can do. But I can also see that our existing business is an accident of fate, in a way. It suited the interests and needs of John and Charlie, but that doesn't mean we have to adapt our futures to the business. If we're smart and thoughtful, we should be able to adapt the business to our futures while still keeping the essential heart of it.

I have been thinking about how different our family's shared purpose for the core capital is, compared to a public company and also compared to other family businesses I know. Making money definitely is important to ensure that the core capital can be sustained, but we're not necessarily money driven. We are looking to strengthen the family and encourage entrepreneurialism, whether that entrepreneurial activity is in the business or outside it.

DRAFT: SHARED PURPOSE OF OWEN FAMILY CORE CAPITAL

- Our capital provides a safety net for our family first and foremost.
- We invest in the ideas of our family members because they will create the enterprise capital of our future.
- We invest in our family relationships because we are stronger together.

Enumerating our core capital and articulating our shared purpose was exciting, but also exhausting. We ended our first day with a good dinner. I don't think we've enjoyed each other's company so much in years. There were still big issues to face, including Mike's concerns about whether he as president would be responsible for delivering all of this, but for the first time we began to see ourselves as a team who could work together.

Christopher Owen

Do I want to be an owner of this business together with my siblings? I have too much to do with my team to focus a lot of time on this stuff. And it is really hard imagining how we're going to make decisions about the business together when I'd rather just get on with things. But I agreed to be here so I'll try to keep an open mind.

Shared Purpose

The shared purpose provides the glue that binds the owners together and keeps them focused on the business and the core capital.

Shared purpose is the answer to the question: Why do we want to be owners of this business together, if at all? Ownership of a business is a choice, and overseeing deployment of core capital is a sufficiently complex undertaking that those who have little time or interest may want to reconsider.

Owners may want to be involved for many different kinds of reasons: a shared commitment to perpetuate a family legacy, a bond around the product or service of the business, a desire to expand their core capital, a desire to create and maintain a safety net that can provide employment, opportunities, or financial support for family members or an entire community.

Particularly for those who inherit their shares, ownership seems more an accident of fate or genetics than a conscious decision and responsibility. Even those who run the business may not take the time to ask themselves why they want to collaborate together with their fellow owners. But understanding *why* is important. The shared purpose provides the glue that binds the owners together and keeps them focused on the business and the core capital.

How does a group of owners articulate their shared purpose? They begin by asking themselves certain key questions:

- What has this business meant to our family over generations?
- What have we as a family invested in it in terms of money, time, effort, opportunities?
- What are our values as a business-owning family and how does the business help us further them?
- How does ownership of the business strengthen—or weaken—our family?
- How does ownership of the business affect our role within the wider community?
- What do I gain from my participation as an owner?
- How much of our collective and individual core capital, in all its forms, is invested in this business?
- Do I want to continue in ownership of this business? What would I gain if I didn't continue? What would I lose?

It is useful for each of the owners to consider the questions on their own, and then to meet to share their answers, beginning with the question, *Why do we want to be owners of this business together?*, and then moving to the other questions. There are no right or wrong answers. The point is to see common threads and then work to articulate them clearly. Contemplating the process can be unnerving—uncovering a lack of shared purpose or a disagreement on the role of ownership might be discouraging. A facilitator with family business experience can help to guide the work and keep discussion on track.

Very often, a shared purpose meeting can be eye-opening: owners discover that their shared purpose is stronger than they imagined and they find a common basis on which to recommit their energies. Shared purpose can reunite and reenergize siblings and cousins who otherwise might not have reason to meet, and foster a new sense of collaboration and consensus.

What if there is no shared purpose? Much of the wealth management industry exhibits a continuity bias: the assumption that it is better for families and owners to stay together and invest together for generations. And for some owners, there is indeed an undeniable shared purpose and sense of collective focus and effort. But for others, shared purpose can be more difficult to articulate, or even nonexistent. When there is a lack of shared purpose, it can be impossible to maintain the energy and focus necessary to sustain engagement, particularly when an owner cannot reach consensus with other owners. Owners who feel bound together against their will run the risk of damaging the business through infighting and inability to work together constructively. In such circumstances, facing up to the reality of the situation with honesty and good intentions can help clarify the path forward.

Sometimes, the answer is to consider seeking exit. One owner may seek to sell or redeem his or her shares individually while the others recommit to going forward. Other times, the other owners may share in the assessment that there is no shared purpose, and the group may consider selling the business, splitting it into several businesses that can be run independently, or disinvesting from it over time by pulling capital from the business to redeploy for other purposes. There is no single right answer: what is important is determining where there is consensus, and where there is not.

Owen Family—January 29, 2012

Amanda Owen Cooper

I was surprised by the discussions yesterday. Having to think beyond financial value to see the different kinds of capital represented by our business and our family helped me broaden my perspective. I want to honor what my parents and grandparents achieved, but I guess I'm coming to see that we don't have to follow in exactly the same path. What we do need to do is make sure we don't waste all our capital. That was the surprising part of the discussion—once we realized all we had at stake, that we could plan our own future, and that we could be stronger together than apart, we began to think more collaboratively.

I am concerned about the trust for Alfred. As trustee, I have a fiduciary obligation to him. We acknowledged that an element of our shared purpose for the core capital is that it will serve as a safety net. But Alfred needs a different safety net from the rest of us. Yes, we depend on the business (particularly Mike and Martha) but we have other sources of income besides dividends to cover our needs.

Alfred's entire future care is riding on the business. I raised the question of whether it might make sense to redeem out the shares held by Alfred's trust and then invest the proceeds in a very stable investment fund. That would protect the nest egg for Alfred while giving Mike and Ryan more room to take some risks to grow the business. Mike immediately began to worry that if we redeemed out one shareholder, wouldn't everyone want cash instead of their shares? Then where would the company be?

It was good to see Mike open up about his concerns around the business, rather than just being strong and silent like our dad. Mike had an opportunity to say that he wants to lead Owen Products but he isn't sure he is up for running the company the way Granddad and Dad ran it, with one president making all the decisions. And we in turn had an opportunity to tell him we appreciate all that he is doing and encourage him to think about how he might organize the company differently. Ideas included getting more management training, reorganizing the existing staff, and running the eastern and western parts of the business as fully separate operations. We also talked a bit about the problems the company is facing right now. Martha offered that Ryan could help Mike if Mike would only let him. Mike started to be defensive about managing the company, and I was worried the discussion would spin out of control, but the facilitator helped Mike and the rest of us talk openly about ideas and possibilities without feeling that we needed to make a decision now or even pass judgment on the ideas. What is important was having the dialog and raising some ideas with the goal of getting ideas on the table before we narrow down the options. If we can come to general consensus about our vision for the business, it will help the board and management build a strategic plan.

We learned a lot about Christopher's work at Eastern University, too, and the potential business opportunities his team is creating. I'd like to see us invest somehow.

Draft: Vision for Owen Products, Ltd. and the Core Capital in 2032

We as owners will oversee all of our capital and not just the financial capital invested in the business. We will have processes in place to enable us to meet this responsibility, keeping in mind our other obligations.

Financial Capital:

- We will sustain and prudently grow the financial capital invested in the business.

- Our personal financial capital is part of the core capital and we will seek to invest it rather than simply spend it.

Human Capital:

- Owen Products will have the management team it needs to achieve its strategic plan. Management will have the abilities and resources to manage the company successfully. Owen Products will endeavor to use our family's human capital judiciously and will avoid shifting all leadership responsibilities to one individual.

- We as family owners will invest our time and energy in educating and preparing the next generation of our family to ensure that they have the skills needed to sustain and grow the core capital inside and outside of the business.

- We will encourage family leadership but recognize that we will be more successful if we also engage the talents and interests of non-family members in leadership positions.

- Owen Products' board will be made up of knowledgeable individuals who bring insight and access to additional resources.

- Owners will be educated and prepared to handle their responsibilities.

- We support family leadership but recognize that we will be more successful if we also engage the talents and interests of non-family members in leadership positions.

Enterprise Capital:

- Owen Products is the engine of Owen family capital. The company will have the resources it needs to continue to operate successfully. The company is in a mature industry. It will strive to build market share but not seek growth-for-growth's sake.

- A substantial part of Owen Products' success has been due to our production and logistics systems, which are the most advanced in our industry. We will invest in maintaining and strengthening this capability and also in developing other ways to leverage this enterprise capital.

- We will encourage Owen family members to create new entrepreneurial opportunities and will consider redeploying enterprise capital from our existing business activities to help fund them. We will have in place a forum to evaluate and support such opportunities.

Draft: Mission for the Owners of Owen Products, 2012–2015

- Create an Owners Council to focus on
  - Refining our understanding of core capital, shared purpose, and vision, especially for capital outside the business
  - Preparing next generation owners to be engaged
  - Ownership succession, especially estate planning
  - Developing a process for evaluating and investing core capital in opportunities outside Owen Products, Ltd.
- Strengthen the board of Owen Products and lay out the owners' vision so that the board can provide effective strategic oversight and support for management and create a board–owner nominating committee.
- Articulate our vision to the board and work with the board to develop a strategic planning process to guide board and management's efforts.
- Encourage the creation of a family council to strengthen family bonds and sustain the Owen legacy.
- Actively monitor and evaluate opportunities to invest core capital in family-generated opportunities.

Michael Owen

Would Dad and Granddad support this vision and mission, or are they rolling in their graves? I think they would support it. I am beginning to see that my fellow owners don't want to meddle in management; they want to help make sure that management has the resources it needs and that the business has a clear direction. I am also beginning to understand the value of thinking about deploying core capital outside the business. The business was everything to my dad and granddad, but given our growing human capital and our enterprise capital, our future can and should be broader than just the business.

CHAPTER

8

Vision and Mission

Vision

> A clear and well-articulated vision animates the shared purpose and creates a sense of mission: the owners can see the future and focus their efforts on achieving it.

Vision is the owners' collective view of the future of the core capital and the business. It is the answer to the question: Now that we can articulate our shared purpose, what is our destination? What future do we see as a result of committing to our shared purpose?

A clear and well-articulated vision animates the shared purpose and creates a sense of mission: the owners can see the future and focus their efforts on creating plans to achieve it. And while the shared purpose belongs to the owners as a group, the vision becomes the vision for the entire business and the core capital: it is the animating driver of the business. The owners' vision frames the board's discussion of strategy. It creates the direction and boundaries for management's deployment of resources. It gives family members an understanding of the purpose and direction of the business. That is why it is important for owners to take the time to articulate their shared purpose and vision. As the owners of the business and the core capital, they are responsible for setting the ultimate, highest level goals for the business. And if they ignore that responsibility or delegate it other groups, then they risk having the business run away with their capital in directions that don't further their shared purpose.

For example, imagine a business with substantial cash reserves. The owners, having experienced business cycles when no bank would lend to the business, see that financial capital as a nest egg that can help them weather financial downturns. But without guidance from the owners, a board (particularly, an independent board well-stocked with veterans of public companies in the industry) may be concerned that the cash is not earning a sufficient return and propose embarking on a series of acquisitions to expand the business's capabilities, betting that the growth will outpace the risk. This is a reasonable strategy from the perspective of a public company, but it is entirely contrary to the shared purpose of these owners. These owners must articulate a vision that sets basic parameters for use of cash reserves to provide guidance to the board and management in their strategic planning work.

How does a group of owners articulate their vision? First, they remind themselves of the core capital and their shared purpose. It is important for the owners to recommit to their shared purpose before embarking on a visioning exercise, especially if time has passed since the shared purpose work. The owners then ask: *What does success look like? What will the business and all its forms of core capital look like in 20 years if we are successful at achieving our vision?*

At the outset, the owners will want to commit to speaking for themselves while acting with respect and maintaining an open mind. Absolute consensus is extremely rare in visioning, and the most positive outcomes come when participants come to the table without preconceptions. As with the shared purpose exercise, it can be helpful to do the visioning work with a facilitator, who can manage the discussion, maintain order, and avoid taking sides.

One member volunteers as scribe. Using a flipchart, the group sets up three separate pages, one for each of the types of core capital. Then, one by one, each member of the group offers up a vision of the future in 20 years for each type of capital: human, social, financial, and business.

Go around the group in a set order, which reduces the risk that one member of the group will dominate the discussion. To maximize the benefit of the exercise, the group must avoid the temptation to judge, criticize, improve, rank, or otherwise evaluate the vision elements during this first pass—the goal is simply to get all the possible elements of the vision out on paper. There is no right or wrong in this exercise.

Each vision is stated as an outcome, rather than a process. The owners may wish to set forth the vision in terms of types of capital:

In 2037:
- Financial capital:
  - The business is financially stable with adequate financial reserves.
  - Owners have built capital other than their shares.
- Human capital:
  - Because the owners have set aside financial capital separate from the business, family members enjoy excellent educations and can depend on family resources in the event of emergency, which frees them to achieve their individual goals.
  - G3 family members have opportunities to work in the business.
  - Because the business is an excellent place to work, it enjoys very low rates of employee attrition.
- Enterprise capital:
  - The business enjoys a reputation as a good citizen of the community.
  - The business has expanded into new markets by harnessing employee knowhow.
  - An entrepreneur's fund started by the owners provides seed capital and technical and startup assistance for business opportunities generated by family members.

Next, the group steps back and looks at each of the core capital pages, one by one. Is there consensus around the vision in each area of core capital? Is the vision clear, or would it benefit from greater detail? Work to bring the vision to three or four points for each type of capital. Review the vision for each of the forms of core capital. Do they align? Give them a reality check: Can they be achieved simultaneously? Do they potentially conflict (for example, "We have substantial capital reserves that enable us to weather ups and downs of the business cycle" and "We have invested our free cash flow in startup opportunities")? If so, is there an acceptable middle ground?

Visioning requires a balance of dream, ambition, and—before the process is finished—healthy skepticism. The ultimate test: Does this vision further the shared purpose?

Mission

The mission is the plan that funnels vision and shared purpose into a high-level strategy to guide the business and ensure the successful deployment of the core capital.

Now that the owners have articulated their shared purpose and vision, the final element of getting organized is to lay out a plan: What do we have to do or become in order to achieve the vision? In essence, the mission is the plan that funnels vision and shared purpose into a high-level strategy to guide the business and ensure the successful deployment of the core capital.

A mission exercise should be undertaken reasonably soon after the visioning exercise, while owners are energized by the vision. Once again, the group will want to begin by revisiting the shared purpose and remembering why they choose to continue as owners of this business and its core capital together.

Next, they review the vision in detail for each of the forms of core capital. The work of the session centers on the question: What must we as the owners do and what must we coordinate with other groups to do to achieve the vision? How will we measure success?

Is there a priority among the elements of the vision? The group should ask itself: Which form of capital is most important? Does this group put financial capital goals first? Enterprise capital goals first? Human capital goals first? What are the potential tradeoffs? For example, if the group wants to invest in human capital of the family by staking family members in their startups, where will that cash come from? Will it come from dividends? What implications would a policy favoring greater dividends have for the capital needs of the business and the expansion opportunities it might generate?

The next question is: What are the steps to achieve this element, and who would undertake them? Working through the answer to this question helps owners see the interplay of the business and the core capital. Some of the steps can only be taken within the business (for example, expanding into new markets) while others can only be taken outside the business (for example, staking next-generation family members in new entrepreneurial ventures in entirely different industries). This exercise thus helps to clarify the future role of the business in the system. Again, the exercise isn't about the business alone. It is about how the activities and decisions regarding the business relate to the future of the human capital and enterprise capital as well as the financial capital.

This is not easy work. If there is no consensus on the vision for a particular type of core capital, or the priorities for the core capital, it is important for the owners to ask: Why not? Where do we differ in our vision? These areas of difference deserve open discussion. What is the scale of the difference? Is it a matter of differing priorities, which could be balanced through thoughtful discussion? Or do the different visions really point to a previously unrecognized misalignment around the shared purpose? The process is iterative; sometimes, if the group is stuck on articulating the mission, it can be helpful to go back and ground the discussion in the shared purpose and vision to bring the group back to consensus.

The goal of the mission exercise is to develop a list of steps that need to be undertaken over the next two to five years to achieve the vision in keeping with the shared purpose. The point is not to develop a strategic plan per se, but rather for the owners to recognize and articulate what needs to happen with respect to the core capital inside and outside the business to reach the 20-year vision. If the vision calls for creating new enterprise capital outside the business (for example, by creating an entrepreneurs' fund to provide seed capital for startup investments launched by family members) and the business is the sole generator of financial capital, then the strategic plan for the business will need to generate harvesting opportunities through either distributions or partial redemptions.

At this point, readers might ask, aren't the owners doing strategic planning that is the responsibility of the board and management? The answer is no: The development of shared purpose, vision, and mission is the work that owners must do in order to define the boundaries of the strategic planning work of the board and management. Leaving the boundaries up to board and management is risky. Board and management may assume that the founder's vision continues uninterrupted. They may assume that the owners will measure performance purely by financial metrics. They may substitute their own vision, or the vision of a public company in the same industry (for example, some board members may assume that owners would want fast growth, or a perfectly level dividend, or being listed in the Forbes 100). In any event, it is highly unlikely that a board will arrive at a strategy that meets the shared purpose and achieves the vision if they don't have input from the owners on what their shared purpose and vision happen to be. Only if the owners do the work of articulating the vision will the board know what to work with management to aim for.

Owen Family—January 29, 2012

Christopher Owen

As I mentioned earlier, I haven't been enthusiastic about these meetings. Ownership seems like a lot of work and involves a lot of time I don't think I'm going to have, given my responsibilities at the university and my new business. Then again, Mike, Martha, and Amanda are my siblings, and Owen Products has been important to my family. And leaving all the work to Mike and expecting big dividends doesn't seem fair, either. Thinking about this core capital idea, can my family help me launch my new business? Do I want them as my partners? Maybe I should sell my Owen Products shares instead so that I have financial capital to invest in my business?

Is the shared purpose and vision for Owen Products good enough? I think it makes sense for Owen Products and the family, and it's feasible. I'm just not sure yet that it's right for me, because I don't know that I can spend so much time and effort. And yet, I am part of the human capital here, and maybe the enterprise capital can help me turn my team's research into a practical business. Would it be right for me to pull away from the family?

Mike Owen

Well, that was interesting. Yes, I have more support than I thought. And we demonstrated that we four siblings can be in a room together for two days and even agree with each other sometimes. But is this the right future for Owen Products? The vision calls for major change in the way we do things. Dad never had to get strategic plans approved by the board or pay attention to what owners wanted. Then again, I know I can't work the way he did. My siblings are sharing the weight with me. Maybe this is a better plan.

Is the shared purpose and vision good enough for me? It works for the business and it's feasible in the real word. I think my siblings are committed, with the possible exception of Christopher. I'm okay with it. Yes, I think so.

Martha Owen Jones

After so much discussion it was a little nerve-wracking to go around the room and find out whether everyone thought the plan was good enough. I found myself really pulling for the plan because it helps my family: Ryan will actually get a real role in the business, I think, and Jameson should have an opportunity inside the business if he still wants it when he graduates, or as an owner. I'm wondering whether it's time to make Ryan an owner, but since he's not bloodline, that may be more than my family can cope with.

I like being part of the business and having a role in making major decisions as an owner. I don't feel like I'm riding in the passenger seat with a blindfold anymore. I am really excited by the possibility of investing in core capital and not just the business. We have a lot of enterprise capital that could be put to work in different ways and we're stronger together. We'll see whether Christopher finds it compelling enough.

Is it good enough? Yes, I think so. I want to make sure we talk about a dividend policy, though. It doesn't make sense that Mike makes a good salary but the owners don't get dividends.

Amanda Owen Cooper

I think this new way of looking at ownership creates a better balance between what the company wants to do and what the owners are willing to invest in. It requires attention, and it's going to be time consuming, but this is our family's capital and we're responsible for it. Doing this work takes some of the pressure off of Mike. I also am kind of excited about the chance to work together with my siblings to see what we can achieve together. So, it's good enough for me.

But it's not good enough for the trust that our uncle Fred created for Alfred. We can't take the kind of risks we may want to take and still make sure he has the money he needs to live on. So, I feel pushed and pulled. I think we're going to need to buy the trust out. But, then again, 25 percent is a big percentage. That raises all kinds of issues that we're going to need to think about: appraisal, terms of sale, and whether Christopher might demand to be bought out if the trust is.

CHAPTER 9

Is It "Good Enough"?

The "Good-Enough" Standard for Consensus

Is it right for me individually?
Is it right for the owner group and the family?
Will it work for the business and for the core capital as a whole?
Is it feasible in the real world?

Enumerating core capital and coming to consensus around a common shared purpose and vision can be tough work, particularly for larger groups. Very rarely will every member find that the results of the group's efforts align perfectly with their own individual purpose and vision, and this is especially true when the ownership group includes one or more directors, members of senior management, trustees, or non-family owners. Reaching consensus in such circumstances can be difficult: Did participants fully evaluate the choices or did they rush to a conclusion or feel forced to decide? Why did they decide as they did?

It can be helpful to test the soundness of the shared purpose and vision and to determine whether consensus has in fact been reached by holding them up against the *good-enough* standard. The good-enough standard for consensus requires an affirmative answer to four questions:

1. Is it right for me individually?
2. Is it right for the owner group and the family?
3. Will it work for the business and for the core capital as a whole?
4. Is it feasible in the real world?

When ownership is held by a group, no plan will fit all the needs and desires of each member of the group perfectly. The good-enough standard helps participants to be reality based and pragmatic in their discussions about an important decision. Owner groups will find it useful to adopt the good-enough standard early on in the process, because it can help group members pinpoint their concerns. By working through the four questions, a participant can think in more concrete terms and thereby bring the discussion around to a particular matter of concern. The standard helps participants to relax and focus, and avoids the tendency to vote a matter up or down too early in the discussion process, because it invites participants to think through and discuss a question from multiple perspectives.

Owen Family—February 21, 2012

Amanda Owen Cooper

My siblings and I had a conference call this morning to talk about the trust for Alfred and what our redemption policy should be in this case. As you know, I am the trustee and have a fiduciary duty to act in his interests and invest the trust assets prudently. I explained my responsibilities and Alfred's health needs: the trust is his primary source of income and pays for expensive residential care. Alfred is in his fifties so it is my responsibility to make sure that the trust assets are invested in a way that secures his long-term future. My siblings agreed that dividends might not be sufficient to fund these needs and that it would be better for the trust's assets to be invested in liquid securities that could be sold as necessary.

To make sure we understood the implications, we talked for a while about how a redemption might work. We would need to get an appraisal for the shares to figure out how much they are worth. Cash is tight at Owen Products right now because of some capital investment being made in the western facility that Dad planned a couple of years ago. (This reminded us that the planning cycle for the business is very long and our vision will take quite a while to work its way through the cycle.) Mike noted that cash on hand is not enough to fund the redemption. The redemption could be funded with bank debt; rates are reasonable right now. Alternatively, the business could pay cash for part of the shares and provide a promissory note secured by some of the assets of the business. We recognize that this is a matter for board approval: we will recommend the redemption but it is the board's responsibility to approve the redemption and to determine the mechanics. I am a member of the board but will abstain from the voting on this topic, since I face a three-way conflict of interest: owner, director, and trustee.

So, if I think about it, what we are doing is pulling financial capital from the business in order to further our shared purpose for the core capital. We all feel this is the right thing to do given family needs, even if it isn't optimal from a business perspective.

We also asked Christopher whether he had decided whether our vision is good enough for him; would he be pursuing redemption of his shares as well? I was worried; if he wanted to redeem along with Alfred's trust, we would have a major financial challenge that could cripple the company. Somewhat to our surprise, he said he had thought about it for a long while, that he wanted to remain an owner, and that he would do his best to uphold his responsibilities.

CHAPTER 10

Alternatives to Engaged Ownership

Not all owners will want to be engaged owners, for all sorts of reasons. Lack of desire or ability isn't failure, but it is a reality that the ownership group will need to face.

Those who become engaged owners focus on recognizing, growing, and sustaining the core capital in all its forms that their ownership represents. Engaged owners who recognize that there is more at stake than money, and bring interest, understanding, ability, and longsightedness and broadsightedness to their role, increase the odds that the family's human capital and enterprise capital as well as its financial capital will be deployed thoughtfully to achieve their shared purpose and vision.

Not all owners will want to be engaged owners, for all sorts of reasons. Lack of desire or ability on the part of an owner isn't failure; rather, it is a reality that the ownership group will need to face. An owner may be too busy and unable to turn away from other obligations to devote the time, commitment, and energy required to be an engaged owner of a business. An owner may be angry or estranged from other owners and unable to set aside deep-seated personal feelings: animosity, jealousy, dislike, or frustration. One owner's system of values and principles may be so different from another's that they will never be able to work together to articulate the owners' shared purpose and vision for the future. An owner may simply not be interested. Or, an owner may be deeply interested but, due to illness, age, or incapacity, unable to take part in the process of ownership decision making that engaged ownership requires. What then?

If the majority of the group is willing, interested, and able to take on the work of engagement, then there are two options that would enable the group to move forward: exit or delegation.

Exit

When there is an owner who cannot or does not want to join in the work and whose interests do not align with the shared purpose and vision, the best option may be an exit, through either cross-purchase (where one or more of the other owners buy out the exiting owner) or redemption (where the business purchases the exiting owner's shares). The process for exit often is laid out in the corporate documents (in particular, the shareholders agreement or buy–sell agreement).

Engaged owners will want to avoid the natural instinct to minimize the exit price paid for the shares. Discounts (whether for minority interest or lack of marketability) should be transparent, fully explained, and applied consistently over similar transactions. The cost in human capital of an aggrieved and angry former shareholder will be much greater over the long term than the savings in financial capital. It is important for controlling owners who intend to transfer their shares to a group to assess whether the group is in fact interested in becoming owners and capable of engagement. Transferring ownership to any individual who cannot or will not participate in group decision making, or to a group that has never been able to see eye-to-eye, sets the group up for failure and can potentially put the business and the core capital at risk. This points out the value of opening up the conversation among generations well before any estate planning takes place; no matter how loving the controlling owner's intention, if the recipients of the shares have no interest in joining together as owners, and no preparation, the plan is likely to sow discord.

Delegation

Another option is for the owner who is unable or unwilling to undertake the work of engagement to delegate the task of engaged decision making to another individual, generally by granting a proxy. This mechanism is particularly effective when the unwillingness or inability is due to some circumstance that is temporary; the owner may be too young, suffering from an illness, or unable to focus on ownership matters due to a major life event such as a divorce, childbirth, or caring for an ill or injured family member. The delegation—the granting of the proxy—should be for a set period (which could be extended if necessary) and the proxy holder will need to shoulder the task of keeping the nonparticipating member reasonably informed of the work of the owners and the decisions they are facing. Otherwise, the owner whose decision making has been delegated may find it overwhelmingly difficult to catch up when his circumstances change and he wants to become engaged.

Other Options

If more than one member of the group is unwilling to take on the work of developing consensus around shared purpose and vision, or the work itself generates disagreement that the group feels is insurmountable, then they will need to consider a different set of options. Being part of a group that cannot find a common identity is uncomfortable and potentially explosive, particularly when the business has been part of the family's universe for generations. The goal in such a situation is to choose an option that is most likely to preserve the members' relationships as a family while also sustaining the core capital. When there is no common shared purpose or vision, the risk of losing core capital is real: the job of the owners in such a circumstance is to reorganize ownership and decision making in some way that can be sustainable over time.

Pruning the Tree

If there is a subset of the group that wants to go forward as engaged owners, while another group wishes to exit, then the group as a whole will want to weigh the cost and benefit of a larger exit. Pruning the tree—engineering a multiparty redemption or cross-purchase that will concentrate ownership in fewer hands—is a common strategy when an owner-manager wants to take the business in a direction that doesn't suit the shared purpose or vision of the rest of the owners. The challenge for the owner-manager who will remain an owner as others exit is to recognize and value what is at stake for those who are selling their shares. The transaction will be challenging from a purely financial perspective (is the selling price fair and are the terms acceptable for both parties and feasible for the business over the long term?). It will also be challenging from a core capital perspective. (Will human capital in the form of family relationships and reputation be harmed? Will selling shareholders have any expectation of future participation in non-financial core capital? For example, will their children be welcomed if they apply to work in the business in the future? Will the business continue to support the same charitable activities that the family as a whole has championed in the past?) Selling shares that represent a family legacy can raise strong emotions, and coming to agreement around the terms of such a deal may be time-consuming and even seem irrational at times. Those who opt to remain as owners will be most successful if they appreciate and respect that those who are selling are coping with issues that go far beyond the finances of the deal.

At the same time, the challenge for the owners who wish to exit is to recognize and value the task that the owner(s) who stay on will face as they continue forward with the business. A redemption or buyout removes human capital as well as financial capital from the business and may impair some of the enterprise capital as well. The exiting owners will have very different interests and concerns, and often will cease to be sounding boards and ready supporters. Often, debt will be taken on to finance the transaction with the result that the business must overcome additional hurdles to achieve profitability. Funding the exit may drain away cash that otherwise would have been used for capital investment strategies; after funding the exit, the business may not be able to make capital improvements, expand its market presence, or acquire additional businesses. The exiting owners will best serve the core capital if they recognize the importance of balancing the cost of the exit with the future needs of the business.

There are a variety of creative ways to structure an exit from a business that can safeguard the business while also achieving an attractive price for the sellers. Payments can be made over time with the sellers taking a security interest, or income-producing assets such as real estate can be spun out. Owners who commit to the exit and then work together to achieve mutually acceptable terms will enhance both their financial and human capital.

Dividing into Silos

Where a business consists of multiple businesses and multiple owner-managers, none of whom can reach consensus around a shared purpose and vision, division of the business may offer a reasonable alternative to engaged ownership. Under a siloed system, the business is separated into divisions or subsidiaries, each of which is run by an owner-manager. Sometimes, the group will agree to common ownership but divided control, leaving most decisions to be made at the silo level and just a few at the corporate level. Just as pruning the tree recreates the controlling owner-led decision-making system that prevailed before ownership was transferred by the former controlling owner, dividing into silos creates a group of divisions, each operated by a different member of the group and with minimal common decision making. Dividing into silos does permit a group of owners to share enterprise capital, including branding/marketing, administrative systems, and/or technical knowhow or R&D. Provided that group is willing to share the benefits and risks of joint ownership, and can deal with making decisions together on a limited and defined set of issues, dividing into silos might be more cost effective than a complete separation.

Spinoff/Splitoff/Splitup

Sometimes when there is no shared purpose and vision, the group may decide to forgo common ownership entirely and choose instead to divide the enterprise into separate, standalone businesses, each owned solely by its controlling owner. This is a more extreme version of dividing into silos, with no common ownership or shared operations. If there is truly no shared purpose, a complete and final division may be a more workable choice than maintaining common ownership. However, dividing into silos makes it more difficult to share enterprise capital, so freedom can come at the expense of core capital.

Sale

If there is no hope or expectation that the owners will reach consensus around shared purpose and vision, and there is no owner willing and able to buy out the others, then, perhaps ironically, sale of the business may be the only option that can preserve financial and human capital for the family, though perhaps with a loss of enterprise capital and human capital within the business. When a business is considered a family member and owners have been told for their entire lives that ownership must stay in the family at all costs, it can be difficult for owners to admit that continued ownership of the business is impossible. But owners who try to keep the business in the family in spite of a lack of shared purpose and vision will find that human capital becomes impaired first, as family, board, and management disagree on the future course of action and relationships begin to fray as a result. Impaired human capital then leads to impaired enterprise capital as poor communication damages systems and processes. Ultimately, the business suffers financially. Coming together for the limited purpose of achieving a successful sale may be difficult, but recognition of all that is at stake—all the human capital and enterprise capital as well as the financial capital—may help generate sufficient consensus.

PART

III

Practicing Engaged Ownership

Owen Family—June 16, 2012

Martha Owen Jones

Today is our first official meeting of the Owen Products' Owners Council. After quite a bit of discussion, we agreed upon the following structure for this forum:

- Goals and tasks:
  - Act in furtherance of the shared purpose and vision.
  - Speak with one voice on issues relating to the business and core capital.
  - Promote effective decision making regarding our family and core capital.
- Membership of the group—all owners of the business. Next-generation family members aged 25 or over may observe at the invitation of the group.
- Leadership:
  - Chair—Martha (we agreed it would be better to choose a chair who doesn't work for the company or sit on the board, if possible)

- ○ Co-chair—Christopher
- ○ Representative to the board—Amanda
- Meetings:
  - ○ Annual 1-day retreat
  - ○ Quarterly 3-hour meeting, two weeks before the board meeting
  - ○ Monthly 1-hour conference call
- Voting: Seek consensus
- Accountability: We agreed to hold ourselves accountable through moral suasion rather than strict legal rules or requirements. We agreed that if a member of the forum has more than two unexcused absences per year, or more than four excused absences, we will reconsider.

We also agreed that we need a Family Assembly so that there will be a forum for discussing family issues related to the business and the core capital, and educating family members. The Family Assembly will give us and our spouses a place to discuss matters as a group (other than during holiday dinners!). We are going to hold the first meeting later this summer when we're all together. We'll help the Family Assembly get organized, and we'll be members, but we don't want to control it. We want it to be an independent group rather than a satellite.

11

Forums

Forums: Board, Owners Council, Family Assembly

Family, owners, board, and management all have their own objectives and perspectives. One of the responsibilities of the owners as the ultimate owners of the core capital is to create opportunities for each group's voice to be heard.

Family business owners are familiar with the problem of business issues popping up at family dinners and family disagreements surfacing at board meetings. Family businesses are complex systems with multiple and interlocking roles and relationships. The ambiguity, intrigue, and shadow decision making that happens when decisions aren't made in the right forum can impede engaged ownership and indeed trip up decision making throughout the family-business system.

Recognizing that each of the groups—family, owners, board, and management—has its own objectives and perspective, one of the responsibilities of the owners as the ultimate owners of the core capital is to create opportunities for each group's voice to be heard. Decision making will be more effective if each group has a forum in which to come together.

The three main forums are the Owners Council, the Board of Directors, and the Family Assembly. Each has its own membership, focus, and responsibilities:

- The Owners Council is responsible for articulating the shared purpose and vision for the business and for the broader core capital. Membership includes all owners, including individual owners and trustees of family trusts that own shares in the business. If there are non-family owners, the Owners Council may choose to include them as well, in part or all of its activities. The Owners Council is responsible for providing a forum to assist owners in making the decisions reserved to the owners. It is also responsible for ownership succession, including preparing the rising generation to become engaged owners. The Owners Council is responsible for the question: *What is our vision for the future of the business and the core capital?*
- The Board of Directors is the overseer of the business. It is composed of directors elected by the owners. While the board's exact responsibilities are determined by the owners, who determine which powers will be reserved to the owners and which will be delegated to the board, generally the board is responsible for serving as the liaison between the business and the owners, for hiring and overseeing management, and for approving the financial and strategic plans of the business. The board is responsible for the question: *How will the business deploy its financial, human, and enterprise capital to achieve the vision set forth by the owners?*
- The Family Assembly is responsible for maintaining effective family relationships—for strengthening the family glue. Membership includes all family members, however "family member" is defined by the family. The Family Assembly may organize family retreats and gatherings. The Family Assembly also may be tasked with preserving the family's values and legacy and for leading the tasks of family education and mentoring. The Family Assembly may take responsibility for family philanthropy. The Family Assembly is responsible for these questions: *How will we preserve and strengthen our family relationships? How will we prepare our descendants to participate effectively in the family business system and to sustain the core capital?*

Senior management will typically create its own forums to handle the work of managing the business on a day-to-day basis.

The owners, operating through the Owners Council, create the initial basic organizational structure for each forum. Often, owners will find that organizational aspects of the board are set forth in the organizational documents of the business (typically, the certificate of incorporation and bylaws or code of regulations) but that there is no equivalent for the Family Assembly and Owners Council. Owners creating a new forum will want to spell out:

- Goals and tasks of the forum
- Membership of the forum
- Leadership structure of the forum (e.g., chair, vice chair, secretary, etc., and how they are appointed) and the style of leadership
- How often the forum will meet, and whether in person or via conference call or video
- How the forum will decide an issue (by consensus, by majority, by supermajority)
- How the forum will determine its agenda and keep a record of its discussions and decisions
- How the members of the forum will hold themselves accountable (and how the forum will be held accountable by the other forums).

These details are set down in writing, along with the mechanism by which the group, once assembled, can amend them to better fit its particular circumstances. The job for the owners is not to carve in stone how the Family Assembly or Board of Directors should do its work, but rather to provide a stable starting point. The gathering of the members of a group is referred to here as a "forum" rather than an "entity" to indicate that it need not have a formal legal existence, though some owners may choose to give a forum legal standing. For example, the Owners Council could be established as a non-stock corporation or LLC and operate in accordance with a charter established with the formation of the entity, or its operations could be spelled out in the shareholders agreement or possibly the bylaws.

The overall objective for each forum is to be able to represent the needs and interests of its constituency, to make those decisions retained by or delegated to it, and to speak with one voice in decision making with other forums. The new forums will operate more effectively if the initial chairs have leadership experience gleaned from participating on a well-run corporate or nonprofit board. At the same time, owners will want to guard against the temptation to name the most experienced member the chair of every forum.

Some owners will name a trusted administrative member of the business or family office staff as secretariat of all groups. The secretariat is responsible for arranging meetings, notifying members, keeping minutes, and distributing information to all the members of each group.

Decision making within the family-business system will operate more smoothly if everyone within the system develops the habit of asking themselves and each other: "Which forum is the right place for me to address this particular question or issue?" (This isn't easy, particularly if everyone within the system grew accustomed to centralized decision making under a controlling owner.) Is this a family question? A business question? An ownership question? To promote discussion, the leader of each forum will want to educate everyone in the system about the forum's focus and encourage communication through the system about its work. More than a few questions will implicate more than one group and may require joint efforts or meetings.

Those who wear multiple hats within the organization—particularly, family-owner-managers—will want to ask themselves, "What hat am I wearing when I consider this particular question?" This is especially important when a business or ownership question arises that affects two or more individuals who are also related—father and son, sister and brother, uncle and niece. In such instances, the participants may find it difficult to consider the issue separate and apart from their personal relationship. This is because familial relationships have been built up over tremendously long periods of time and may be reinforced by multigenerational values (for example, being deferential to elders). However, when it comes to making decisions about the business and the core capital, too much deference may result in a failure to look closely at what truly is at stake.

Another important habit for building engaged ownership and effective system-wide decision making is developing a collective understanding of which decisions will be made on a day-to-day basis by management and which belong to a forum. Engaged ownership should never become meddling. For a business to function effectively, most day-to-day decision making and even much strategic planning will necessarily happen at the managerial level. Otherwise, the business will stagnate while owners and board debate who should plow the drive or choose the paint color for the reception area, or, less facetiously, determine what capital investment will be necessary to maintain market share or develop a human resources and compensation program. Engaged ownership has to overcome the tendency toward centralized decision making (and possibly, micromanagement) that operated under the founding owner. To avoid micromanaging and to further the owners' shared purpose and vision, a critical task for owners is redefining the allocation of decision-making power among family, owners, board, and management in service of sustaining and growing the core capital.

Owen Family—September 18, 2012

Michael Owen

At our quarterly Owners Council meeting yesterday, we did some work around which forums or individuals should make which decisions. Before we started working on engagement, I never would have thought about this question: my dad ran the company and made all the decisions, so when the board named me president I figured I would have the same role. I confess that I was put off by the notion of sharing decision making with the owners, much less with the board. My dad was always careful to organize board meetings so he could make sure the board would agree with whatever plan he had in mind. And he was the only owner, so ownership questions never entered the picture. Besides, don't our bylaws spell all this stuff out? Amanda explained that the corporate law of our jurisdiction spells out some requirements, but privately held businesses have a great deal of leeway in how they choose to govern themselves.

At the beginning of the meeting, I just wanted to make management responsible for everything—just leave us alone to get on with running the business, thank you! I felt that everyone was doubting my motives and my ability. But then Martha asked me to think about what decisions I would want to make if we were going to make a big investment in a new business started by her son, Jameson, and that started me thinking. Jameson is a smart kid, and I'm sure his ideas would be good. But if I were investing in his business, I wouldn't want to go in blind. I'd want access to financial information. I'd certainly want to vote on the directors. I'd probably want to be part of the nominating committee that put together the slate of directors. I'd want some say about how much debt the business could take on, since debt holders would be first in line if the business went bankrupts or were dissolved down the line. I'd want to know what the business strategy is, not so much to control it or judge it, but to understand what the business is trying to do and whether it is sticking to the strategy that was proposed when I invested. And I'd want some say in how shareholders can transfer their shares, and who they can transfer them to, and whether the company can issue more shares. Once I got thinking about all this, I understood my sisters' and brother's interest in this topic: ownership questions are very different from management questions. As owners, we too have a lot at stake.

Allocating Power among Owners, Board, and Management

Thinking about the Allocation of Decision-Making Power

> Owners sit at the center of business decision making from the moment the business is created. The question is: What will the owners choose to do with their power—keep it or delegate it?

All decision-making power within a corporation initially belongs to the owners. This may seem counterintuitive in a business world where CEOs and their management teams are the face of corporate strategy and decision making, but owners sit at the center of business decision making from the moment the business is created. The question is what owners will chose to do with their power. Under the public company model, owners generally delegate nearly all decision making except for the right to vote for a slate of directors, to approve the auditor, and the right to approve certain major transactions (such as a sale of the business or substantially all its assets). This system has arisen in response to the popularity of the public company model, where a large and diverse group of owners are making a financial investment, few if any hold a controlling interest, and those who are unhappy with management's decision making can choose to exit by selling their shares in a well-regulated public market.

Government statutes and codes provide a basic default structure for private corporation decision making that is very much in keeping with the public company model. Engaged owners should recognize that these same statutes do not mandate that a company put in place the default framework; rather, these statutes and codes generally offer opportunities for very different allocations of power and thereby permit customized structures for reallocating decision-making power in ways that might better suit the needs of a particular family and business. At one end of the spectrum, the owners can retain all powers and control all decisions, and this is the model we see in very small one-person businesses. Founder-run or controlling-owner businesses typically exhibit some degree of delegation to a board and management, but they hew closely to the single central decision-maker model as well. Yet, these models can become inefficient as the business grows, and can leave non-managing owners completely in the dark. What other options exist between the controlling owner/centralized decision-making model and the public company model?

For engaged owners who have enumerated their core capital and articulated a shared purpose and vision, and have begun the work of creating forums for family, business, and ownership discussion and decision making, the task is to allocate decision-making power in a way that gives the owners a voice in the highest level of strategic decision making, and the family a voice in issues that affect them, while still giving the board and management sufficient leeway to operate the business.

Building an Allocation Grid

> Retaining the right to approve the strategic plan may be the most valuable right the Owners Council can retain.

The Owners Council begins the work of allocating power among owners, board, and family by developing a list all of the key decisions that might need to be made. Their list might include the following (for a more detailed list, see the appendix):

- Acquire a new business.
- Change the brand.

- Elect the board.
- Borrow money.
- Hire family members.
- Hire the CEO.
- Declare a dividend.
- Approve the annual plan.
- Approve the five-year strategic plan.
- Approve the auditor.
- Sell the business.
- Move the headquarters.
- Reduce the workforce by more than X percent.
- Change the employee benefit plan substantially.
- Increase or decrease corporate-level charitable giving by more than Y percent.
- Determine the qualifications to be an owner and establish share transfer restrictions.
- Redeem shares.

What is probably clear from even this incomplete list is that the owners' shared purpose and their vision for the future of the business and for the deployment of the core capital will affect, and possibly even dictate, the outcome of each of these decisions. How these decisions are made and implemented matters to the owners and the family, quite likely in ways that a financially focused investor might not notice or care about. For example, reducing corporate-level charitable giving might be an entirely logical way for a cash-strapped company to fund capital investments. But for a business that is viewed by the community as a prominent citizen, such a change, if not thoughtfully announced and, perhaps, coordinated with an increase in family-level giving, might irrevocably damage the business's—and the family's—reputation and standing in the eyes of the community. Likewise, the choice of CEO will have implications not just for the leadership of the business, but also for the owners and for the family. The CEO isn't just the leader of the business; he or she is the voice and public face of the business and, in many circumstances, of the family as well. A CEO who makes decisions based purely on financial criteria without considering the impact on human capital and enterprise capital may increase the value of the business and its standing among its peer companies, but may so discourage and frustrate employees that innovation is stifled and the business struggles in the future.

So what does this mean for allocating decision-making power? The job for the owners is to consider whether the default system spelled out in the company's bylaws and day-to-day practice works for them, and, if not, which group(s) should make the key decisions. Once they have completed the list of critical decisions, the owners should create a grid, with the decisions running down the left-hand column and the decision-making forums (Owners individually, Owners Council, Board of Directors, Management, Family Assembly) across the top.

The first step is to highlight the block in the grid to show which group (or individual) currently holds the power to decide. They may need to consult with the board or corporate counsel to determine this; they may also want to add another column to provide space for detailing how a decision is made currently (or how it was made immediately before the ownership transfer). This is important because the owners may find any number of decisions that are still made by someone who is influential but holds no formal power—the retired founder of the business or the matriarch of the family, for example.

Then, the owners complete the grid by filling in the cells as follows:

D = Power to decide

C = Right to be consulted before another group with the power to make a decision acts

V = Power to veto a decision made by another group

A = Power to set the decision-making agenda

I = Right to be informed promptly after a decision is made by another group

The rules for the exercise are relative simple:

- Every row must have one (and only one) D.
- Every row may have a C, a V, an A, and/or an I.

In thinking about allocating powers, the owners will want to keep a number of factors in mind:

- Certain decisions, such as whether to sell or dissolve the business, are so fundamental that they belong to the owners individually. The Owners Council can serve as an important forum for educating the owners and providing a forum for discussion around those issues before the individual owners make their vote.

- Other fundamental decisions—whether to sell all or a substantial part of the business, or borrow money over a certain threshold, or change the dividend policy—that affect the ability to achieve the owners' vision and could irrevocably change the future deployment of the core capital inside and outside the business merit consideration by engaged owners *as a group*. The owners will want to consider whether to delegate the ultimate decision to the Owners Council or to maintain the right to decide on an individual basis.

- Retaining a specific power will give the Owners Council control of that decision, but also the responsibility to make it on a timely basis. Thus, retaining the right to make a given decision may slow down business decision making at critical times, particularly when none of the owners are involved in day-to-day operations and lack the information needed to make a decision that must be made quickly. This suggests that delegating the right to decide to the board while retaining the right to be consulted may enable owners to balance their need for information with the realities of short-fuse corporate decision making.

- Beware of the impulse to share decision making among forums (for example, between the owners and the family). By all means, share discussion and deliberation around critical decisions among the forums; indeed, consider holding multi-forum meetings to share information and viewpoints on the most critical issues. Ultimately, though, one group must bear the responsibility of making a decision; sharing that responsibility raises the real risk that the decision will be passed back and forth and never finally made, to the detriment of the business and the core capital.

- Similarly, when the Owners Council retains a power to decide it may create a disincentive for another group to think creatively and proactively about the issue. Delegating the right to decide to the board but keeping the right to be consulted may give the owners the influence they seek without disengaging the board and management from the process.

- Likewise, for decisions that could have a tremendous impact on the entire family, the right to be consulted may be given to the Family Assembly.
- For critical decisions that may have an outsized impact on the core capital outside as well as inside the business, the Owners Council may wish to retain the right to veto a decision that another group otherwise has the power to make. Be mindful that a veto power is more radical than a consent right. It is akin to the emergency brake on a speeding train; it is a very useful tool in an emergency, but it is difficult to execute without causing collateral damage to the relationship between the two groups.
- Retaining the right to approve the strategic plan for the business may be the most valuable right the Owners Council can retain. Retaining the right to approve the strategic plan is a major shift toward engagement and away from the public company model of corporate decision making, and it reflects the owners' recognition that the strategic plan has an outsized impact on the core capital over time. This emphasizes the importance for engaged ownership of insisting that board and management adhere to an established strategic planning process and schedule. A strategic plan puts in place agreed-upon boundaries for management, board, owners, and family decision making and will reduce the occurrence of emergency decision making.
- The right to set the decision-making agenda is critical but undervalued. Generally, the group that has the power to make a decision would also have the power to set the agenda for that decision. However, the Owners Council might choose to share the right to set the agenda with another group on a critical issue—for example, sharing the right to determine how much of the company's free cash flow will be allocated to capital reinvestment, and how much to dividends, with the board—to ensure adequate education and discussion around the issue take place among board and owners before the decision is made.

  Another example would be the process of agenda setting for the annual meeting of shareholders. This task is often delegated to the company's administrative team or to corporate counsel. Engaged owners instead will recognize that face-to-face meetings with board and senior management are important and relatively rare, and will want to use that time not only to take care of corporate formalities but also to review the shared purpose and vision and update the board and management regarding the ongoing work of the Owners Council and Family Assembly, and vice versa. By retaining the right to set the agenda for the annual meeting of shareholders, the Owners Council can ensure that matters of importance to them are duly considered.

- Another undervalued power is the right to be informed about a decision promptly after it has been made. Knowing what has been decided by other groups helps to keep group decision making current and effective. If the board and management know that they must inform the Owners Council promptly regarding a given decision, they will have an added incentive to follow a thorough decision-making process.
- Some decisions do lend themselves to intergroup decision making. For example, the nominating committee might include representatives from the Owners Council as well as the Board of Directors (and possibly management). In these circumstances, a committee composed of members of each group can be created, and the power to decide then delegated to the committee.
- Other decisions may be framed as policies (for example, family employment policy, or dividend policy). A policy establishes boundaries for ongoing decision making on a given topic and can usefully reduce the incidence of one-off decision making.

Once the decision grid exercise has been completed, the Owners Council will want to look at the grid as a whole and ask themselves: Do the retained powers align with the owners' collective shared purpose and vision?

Once the decision grid exercise has been completed, the Owners Council will want to look at the grid as a whole and ask themselves some questions. Do the retained powers align with the owners' collective shared purpose and vision? They will want to compare the decision grid allocation with the original allocation as expressed in the company's corporate documents: Does the decision grid allocation represent an evolution or a revolution? Is the allocation sensible? Is it feasible? How will it be accepted by the other forums? The consequences of changing the decision-making status quo are not immediately obvious, and the Owners Council would be well-advised to inform the Board of Directors and the Family Assembly of their ideas before the allocation of decision-making powers is finalized.

A group of enthusiastic engaged owners initially may want to retain many decision-making powers. Upon reflection and review, they may come to recognize that they as an Owners Council simply do not have the requisite knowledge or are unable to invest the time that would be necessary to build the knowledge and experience to make so many critical decisions wisely. They may then choose to adjust their own role with respect to a given power down to a consent right, or opt instead to retain a right to be informed, recognizing that requiring board and/or management to keep owners informed may be enough to trigger the implementation of a more thorough and transparent decision-making system at the board and management level.

Ultimately, if the newly proposed allocations of decision-making power represent a substantial change from the current allocation expressed in the shareholders agreement or other corporate documents, they will also want to discuss their thinking with counsel and plan for the amendment of these documents.

Owen Family—December 22, 2012

Amanda Owen Cooper

Today was the first annual board–owner lunch, which followed the quarterly board meeting. We added the lunch to our annual calendar because we want to have an opportunity to meet more casually with our board, and also to thank them for their service on behalf of Owen Products, Ltd. The board has been very respectful of the shareholders' efforts to organize the Owners Council, especially when we presented our thoughts on how decision making should be allocated among family, owners, board, and management. We helped them understand our shared purpose and vision, and the way we value our core capital. They in turn made a number of useful suggestions and helped us understand better the value and perspective they bring to the business as directors.

Over lunch, our newest director, who runs a third-generation family-owned ceramic tile manufacturing company in the West, told us all a story about decision making in his business. Apparently, his cousin, a lawyer who owns 20 percent of the shares, proposed to amend the shareholders' agreement to prohibit share transfers without the consent of a supermajority of 75 percent of the shareholders. His idea was that the owners needed to have the ability to control who would own the shares, to ensure that shares would pass only to those who demonstrated the necessary ability. He was quite adamant about the proposal and created considerable family strife advocating for it. Another cousin, who also held 20 percent, felt equally strongly that owners should have the right and ability to transfer shares to whom they please, provided that the successors were family members. The second cousin's reasoning was twofold: first, supermajority votes give veto power and permit a small group to hold up the entire body, often for personal reasons. Second, the voting rule didn't create any mechanisms to help create education opportunities to ensure that there would be capable owner candidates. Ultimately, the group followed the second cousin's lead and agreed to permit free transfers within the family, and to create a family council to focus on educating family members about the business and responsibilities of ownership. At the end of the story, the director said he had learned that authoritarian rules aren't a particularly good way to govern something as changeable as a family-owned business, and if we Owens can continue to focus on engagement and reaching consensus, he feels we we stand a better chance of being successful over the long term.

CHAPTER 13

Working with Other Forums

Engaged owners don't operate in a vacuum.

Engaged owners don't operate in a vacuum. Their work is intended to take into account the needs and wishes of the wider family and to guide the work of the board and management. Once the groups are defined and the forums—Family Assembly, Owners Council, Board of Directors—are created, the work begins.

For a group of owners just beginning the work of engagement, the first step will be getting the Owners Council and Family Assembly up and running.

Engagement with the Family Assembly

When the Owners Council needs information and guidance about the family's wishes and needs, a strong Family Assembly with respected leadership will be trusted by the family to represent its interests promptly and accurately.

Family Assemblies vary widely. Some boast vibrant leadership, 100 percent family participation, and well-subscribed group activities such as family retreats, picnics, parties, newsletters, webpages, and educational events. Others are smaller forums with more limited engagement—perhaps an annual family gathering. Clearly, an active and inviting Family Assembly can be a tremendous asset for a family and for engaged owners of a family business, because it can achieve stature as the voice of the family. When the Owners Council needs information and guidance about the family's wishes and needs, a strong Family Assembly with respected leadership will be trusted by the family to represent its interests promptly and accurately.

Cross-membership between the Family Assembly and the Owners Council can be very useful, at least at the start. However, to be effective, the Family Assembly needs to be more than the little sibling (or worse, the mouthpiece) of the Owners Council, so cross-leadership is best avoided. Multigenerational leadership of the Family Assembly can be powerful and effective. Often, the owners of a family business will be older members of the family, with established leadership roles: parents, trustees, directors, senior management. The Family Assembly offers the opportunity to give the rising generation a way to participate in organizing family events, thereby building their leadership skills and helping to prepare them for other roles in the family-business system over time and giving the existing leadership a chance to see them in action and provide direction, mentorship, and encouragement.

For families that already have a Family Assembly in place, and where the separate tasks of ownership have not been delineated, the Owners Council faces a delicate task. It must introduce itself as a separate forum that represents the owners' shared purpose and vision to the business and considers how the owners' core capital should be deployed over time, and it must (gently) separate ownership decision making from family decision making. Separating the Owners Council from the Family Assembly may well have the salutary effect of clarifying for the wider family what decisions will be made by whom, and reducing the conflict that can arise when an issue is raised in a forum that has no power to deal with it.

While the Owners Council will want to avoid any suggestion that it controls the Family Assembly, it will want to have an active and visible role. The Owners Council may opt to fund or subsidize the Family Assembly's activities, or sponsor events (such as a family dinner following the shareholders' annual meeting). The Owners Council will also want to volunteer to sponsor and/or provide education about the business and the core capital with the goal of building an understanding among the wider family of all the forms of capital invested in the business.

In turn, the Family Assembly will provide critical information about the family. The Family Assembly can help the owners understand how the family articulates its *family purpose* (the answer to the question: Why do we want to remain closely connected as a family?), values, and goals and how it sees the business and the core capital in service of the family purpose. This information is not static; it changes over time as the family grows and the family's core capital expands. Information gleaned from the Family Assembly can be woven into the shared purpose and vision that owners articulate to the board and management.

This raises the question: Why isn't the owners' statement of shared purpose sufficient? Where the Owners Council is made up of family leaders, does the involvement of a strong Family Assembly create an opportunity for conflict of vision that would not have arisen had the Family Assembly not been organized? This is a problem sometimes faced by family businesses where the family has grown while ownership has remained concentrated, and where the owners' values are less relevant to (or possibly not even accepted by) the broader family group. The Owners Council can choose how involved it wishes to become in the Family Assembly, and how much it wishes to acknowledge and absorb the wider (and changing) family purpose in its own shared purpose and vision. That is indeed the prerogative of the owners. But if the family group includes those who will be the future owners of the core capital, the owners may find that entering into dialog with those who will come next can enrich, rather than weaken, the shared purpose and help both groups find common ground. Making the effort to understand the Family Assembly's perspective may reduce the odds of a revolutionary change in the shared purpose when the ownership changes hands and instead offer the possibility of evolutionary change that won't destroy or waste core capital.

Engagement with the Board

An Owners Council that seeks to build a collaborative relationship and two-way dialog with the board is more likely to be successful in achieving its vision for the business and the core capital.

While the Family Assembly may be an entirely new forum, the business most likely already has a Board of Directors with well-established practices and a working relationship with management. The task, then, for the Owners Council is to introduce itself, the shared purpose, and the vision in a way that promotes dialog and collaboration with the board. Where the board includes owners, the process likely will be easier to begin than where the board consists entirely of independent directors, because owner-directors will already understand the process (and may have begun the work of introducing the concept of engaged ownership to the independent directors). In companies that heretofore were run by a controlling owner or followed the public company model, the task may be more difficult. Rarely is a board actively hostile to an Owners Council (after all, the owners elected the directors and the directors' job is to look after the owners' interests) but the board may find dealing with engaged owners somewhat off-putting, especially if the owners' vision suggests a major realignment of the business strategy is necessary, or the Owners Council is looking to substantially reallocate decision-making powers.

The Owners Council will want to introduce the shared purpose, vision, and decision grid to the board deliberately and over time, and to get the board's feedback. (As a matter both of law and of good practice, the board may also wish to formally acknowledge and/or approve at least some allocations of decision-making power proposed by the owners. Given its fiduciary obligations to the company and the owners, the board may also be obligated to question whether the shared purpose, vision, and decision grid unreasonably constrict its decision-making options.) When a board has been assuming the owners' wishes regarding the optimal deployment of business capital, the delivery of a new vision can disrupt planning. The process of reviewing an existing strategic plan against a new set of goals—as may happen when the Owners Council first introduces its vision to the board—can be time consuming, and owners and board alike will want to take time to consider the implications of the shared purpose, vision, and decision grid. The Owners Council will need to recognize that most businesses more closely resemble an ocean liner than a speedboat: it can take time—possibly years—to completely adjust the strategic plan to align with a different shared purpose and vision.

Take, for example, a chain restaurant business that has built substantial capital reserves. Management and the board may well have developed a strategic plan that calls for deploying those reserves to expand the business. For the sake of this example, we'll assume the business, which has been run by non-family management since the unexpected death of the founder 10 years ago, owns 40 restaurants under three different franchise agreements. The five-year strategic plan approved by the independent board three years ago calls for building up reserves sufficient to enable the company to expand into hotels. Now, assume that the founder's children, who inherited ownership of the company but pursued their own interests rather than join the management of the company, are now in their fifties. Wishing to become more engaged in the ownership of the business their father created, the owners have formed an Owners Council. The Owners Council's shared purpose includes sustaining the existing business while expanding the core capital outside the business by "investing in the savvy of the family lineage," and the vision calls for identifying and investing in entrepreneurial opportunities brought forward by family members. In working with the Family Assembly, the newly created Owners Council has discovered that one of the founder's grandchildren has started up a food safety technology business that, if successful, would revolutionize the restaurant industry. The Owners Council recognizes that the hotel expansion opportunity is likely less risky, from a financial standpoint, but financial investment in the grandchild's food safety technology company would be more likely to further the shared purpose and vision.

In such an instance, the newly minted Owners Council might come forward to the board at the annual shareholders' meeting with a recommendation for increased dividends for the purpose of generating financial reserves outside the business sufficient to fund the grandchild's startup outside the business. If the board and management had already begun moving forward with plans to acquire a hotel franchise in keeping with the strategic plan, such a demand could waste financial and enterprise capital—especially if the company is forced to back out of a hotel franchise contract—and also damage the nascent relationship between the Board of Directors and the Owners Council. Alternatively, the Owners Council, after presenting its shared purpose and vision to the board at a previous meeting, and requesting that the board take this information into account in its planning, might ask the board and management how the strategic plan could be adjusted to accommodate the new shared purpose and vision, and then raise the possibility of the startup investment.

The latter course of action—where the Owners Council prepares the Board of Directors well in advance of their intention to become more engaged, educates the board about its shared purpose, vision, and consequences for future deployment of the core capital, and then requests a change in strategy to accomplish these objective—is more likely to be successful over the long term. In a real sense, it is also an example of how enterprise capital is created, because the board, now that it understands the Owners Council's shared purpose and vision, can be the owners' partner in their effort. (One might even say that the board is only now taking on its original and intended role.)

Some directors may resist, arguing that this new focus on the Owners Council's shared purpose and vision is not what they signed up for when they joined the board and that the new path won't take advantage of their skills and experience. Others may feel that the new vision isn't sufficiently compelling to warrant their time. And indeed, the roster of directors may need to change to accommodate the efforts of the Owners Council. Owners should not take this personally, or as a criticism of their efforts, so long as they have been respectful and open-minded in their discussions with the board. Still other directors might have ideas about how the vision might be accommodated, but via a different path than the one envisioned by the Owners Council. For example, the directors may not have known about the grandchild's startup and may want to learn more with the possible goal of providing corporate funding for the enterprise, which could provide a more tax-effective way to redeploy financial capital than via making distributions. The directors may be able to supply support and assistance through industry introductions or help with technical hurdles the family entrepreneur is encountering. The point here is that an Owners Council that seeks to build a collaborative relationship and two-way dialog with the board is more likely to be successful in achieving the vision.

The Owners Council may also find opposition from non-family senior management for similar reasons. Three things are worth mentioning in this regard:

1. While the Owners Council's ultimate goal is to foster alignment between the work of the board and management, on the one hand, and the shared purpose and vision of the Owners Council on the other, this may not be a quick-and-easy

process, especially when management has operated without the active input of engaged owners for years or even decades. The Owners Council should not expect instant acceptance or understanding and it should avoid using its powers to force change unilaterally.

2. In nearly all companies, it is the board's responsibility to oversee management, not the owners'. Therefore, when accomplishing the Owners Council's vision will require a change of strategic direction within the business, it is the responsibility of the Owners Council to educate the board, and the board's responsibility to educate, direct, and motivate management. Even if the individual owners know management well, they will want to be extremely careful not to overstep their bounds and usurp the board's role. Likewise, the owners individually and as a council will want to avoid at all costs the temptation to tell management what to do or to meddle in management issues. This hands-off policy can be challenging in family businesses with a convivial culture where owners and management socialize together.

3. Above all, the Owners Council will want to remember that its tools are very powerful but also very blunt: owners have the decision-making powers they have retained, but no more. If management ultimately opposes the owners' efforts, shared purpose, and vision, then it is up to the board to take such action as is necessary to bring about realignment. If the board refuses or is unable to do so, the Owners Council may ultimately find it necessary to change the board.

Owen Family—June 6, 2013

Christopher Owen

It has been two years since Dad died. All in all, it is good that I decided to remain as an owner of the business. It hasn't always been easy to own a company with my siblings, because we all see the world differently. I do have to admit, it has been good training for structuring my own business. I've been working on a business plan for a business I call CombuSynth, which will do combustion synthesis of nanoscale catalysts for use in solar cell technology. My grandfather used coal to fire the company's kilns; my dad used natural gas, but our work helps to harness the sun. Working on the engagement process for Owen Products has given me a better sense for what my investors might demand—and why—and how we can structure the board for the new business. I am less interested in going public quickly because I can now see the value of having investors who are involved in setting the vision for the company and working together in different capacities—owners, board, management—to achieve it, rather than just having a financial interest. That said, CombuSynth is not going to be built to be a privately held business for the long term. The industry is too large and is moving too quickly for a small private company to keep up. Instead, we will build the business around an exit strategy of going public or selling to a larger company within a decade.

A colleague asked me what our Owen Products Owners Council meetings are like. I told him the schedule, frequency, and agenda, which made him whistle in surprise. Now he understands what I do with my vacation days. I've come to value the work of getting to consensus. When we started, I was impatient and inclined to take everything to a vote. Now, I see that we make better decisions if we work toward consensus, because the dissenters usually have good ideas that can make the majority's idea work better. I have proposed that we do two of our quarterly meetings via videoconference when we are in different parts of the country, which will use our time more efficiently.

14

Meetings

Meetings

The work of forums is done in meetings. The quality of forum decision making depends on the quality of the meetings that precede the decision.

The work of forums is done in meetings—often in person, other times via video or telephone. The quality of forum decision making depends on the quality of the meetings that precede the decision. The leaders of the Family Assembly and Owners Council may want to keep the following suggestions in mind as they undertake the work of bringing the forums from concept to reality.

Frequency

How often should the Family Assembly and the Owners Council meet? The short answer is: often enough for the group to build the rapport, knowledge, and decision-making skills to do the forum's work effectively.

As a general matter, it is helpful for forums to meet at least annually, to give their members an opportunity to develop the interpersonal relationships necessary to foster consensus building. Many Owners Councils meet semiannually; others, quarterly. An Owners Council seeking to build engagement will likely want to meet relatively frequently, especially at the outset, to develop the shared purpose and vision and to take stock of the core capital. Beyond those recommendations, frequency of forum meetings will depend on what decision making the forum is responsible for and how much education and preparation is necessary to ensure that the group can make those decisions quickly enough to meet the needs of the business.

The more powers a forum retains that affect day-to-day or year-to-year business decision making (as opposed to powers that apply to major onetime events, such as the decision to sell the business), the more often it will likely need to meet. For example, assume the Owners Council retains the right to be consulted on corporate borrowing above a given threshold. If management and the board are considering borrowing, the Owners Council will need to understand the company's financials and financial situation, the reasons for the proposed borrowing, the terms of the loan, and the projections for repaying it. They also need to understand what alternatives exist and what the consequences might be if the company doesn't borrow the funds. All of this suggests that meetings will need to be scheduled so that the board (or, at the board's delegation, management) can present the issue to the Owners Council, and the Owners Council can discuss it before the board makes the final decision.

Family Assemblies often focus their work on strengthening family relationships through various activities. Likewise, where a right to be consulted on a given issue is allocated to the Family Assembly (for example, regarding a change of corporate name or branding), the Family Assembly will need to meet to prepare its members so that they can provide useful feedback to the board.

Quorum and Proxies

It is the forum's prerogative to determine whether it will require a quorum—a minimum number of attendees—for decision making, and whether it will permit a participant who is unable to attend to appoint a proxy to vote in his or her stead. Requiring a quorum will create an incentive for members to participate; permitting proxies will increase flexibility for participants with busy lives and multiple obligations. However, if too many participants opt to appoint a proxy rather than participate in the meeting, the forum may fail or come to resemble a fiefdom, thereby diminishing engagement.

Meeting Guidelines

A forum will achieve better attendance and participation if its leaders follow basic guidelines:

1. Set the meeting schedule well in advance—preferably annually—so that members can plan for meetings. This is particularly important where participants must travel to attend.
2. Establish a meeting agenda, send it out in advance, and follow it. Keep minutes.
3. Provide meeting materials well in advance. Establish an expectation that participants will read materials in advance of the meeting and be prepared for discussion and decision making. This is particularly important for a forum that retains decision-making powers that are critical to the operation of the business.
4. Coordinate the meetings with meetings of other forums (particularly when some members participate in more than one group). For example, hold an Owners Council meeting in the morning and a Family Assembly meeting in the early afternoon on the day before a family retreat begins.
5. Create a simple code of conduct and reinforce it. If the group is unable to function effectively, ask whether the issue is a lack of group discussion/decision-making skills or a lack of alignment around shared purpose and vision. Group discussion/decision-making skills can be improved by bringing in a facilitator. Where there is a lack of alignment around shared purpose or vision, the forum may want to revisit the work it did when it was first created.

Agendas

An agenda sets boundaries and manages participant expectations for the meeting. The agenda should be developed and sent to forum members in advance of the meeting, and the chair should make every effort to keep to the agenda.

The chair of the forum may want to consider establishing an agenda cycle, at least for the first several years of the forum's existence. The purpose of the agenda cycle is to ensure that the forum's members are educated on relevant topics and prepared to make the decisions for which they are responsible. The decision-making responsibilities of the forum should drive the agenda. For example, an agenda cycle for an Owners Council that has agreed to meet quarterly, including a one-day annual retreat, might look like this:

June—Quarterly Meeting (2 hours):

- Business update.
- Forum education: Presentation on the business's strategic plan.

December—Quarterly Meeting (2 hours):

- Business update.
- Forum education: Review board performance and bios of director candidates proposed by nominating committee.
- Forum decision-making: Develop agenda for Annual Meeting of Shareholders.

June—Annual Retreat (7 hours):

- Annual meeting of shareholders:
- Decision-making: Vote on slate of directors, approve auditor.
- Provide update to board on activities of Owners Council.
- Consultation: Board provides update on strategic plan.

Adjourn and Convene Owners Council:

- Discussion: Review of shared purpose and vision—*are we in alignment?*
- Review of core capital—*has the core capital expanded or contracted during the year?*
- Forum education: Discuss shareholder succession plan.
- Forum education: Communication skills training.

September—Quarterly Meeting

- Business update.
- Forum education: Estate planning strategies.
- Forum decision making: Review share transfer policies and shareholders' agreement.

There is considerable flexibility when it comes to forum agenda setting. What is important is to make sure that members receive the information they need to consider well in advance of the date the decision is required.

Participation by Non-members

A forum may operate on a members-only basis, or it may choose to invite presenters, participants, and/or observers. Attendance at forum meetings can be an opportunity for younger family members to see engagement in action and to learn more about the business and how decisions are made. The chair should be clear whether the non-member may participate in discussion or is expected to observe quietly.

Owen Family—December 24, 2013

Mike Owen

Today was challenging but productive. The Owners Council worked over the past month or so to develop a draft policy regarding distributions and investments in new business ventures. The policy calls for making an annual distribution of $10 per share or 20 percent of free cash flow, whichever is greater. There are 50,000 shares outstanding and the $10-per-share minimum means that if the dividend policy is implemented, the company will be required to distribute a minimum of $500,000 per year. The policy also calls for creating a pool of capital within the company that will be available for making acquisitions and investments—we called it a war chest.

These policies are a big change for us. Dad began paying dividends after his Uncle Fred retired, since it was the only way to get him some income, but the amounts varied from zero in tight years to $20 a share in 2007, a year when we had extra-high sales. There was never really a *policy*. I remember that Dad would spend a couple of hours with his pocket calculator the night before the annual meeting figuring out what the dividend should be. His system was certainly flexible, but I can see the value of adding certainty. I've gotten really tired of having my siblings call me or our CFO in late November or early December to ask us what we think the dividend will be. Then again, I don't want to be distributing money if the business needs it. That said, board has helped me understand that Owen Products' financial capital isn't free and that the shareholders who make it available to us deserve a return. Can you tell that I'm torn between thinking like an owner and thinking like the president (and a board member!) of the company?

So today, the Owners Council brought the proposal to the board for discussion and debate. The board had a lot to say about the draft policy:

- Generally, the board supports implementing a dividend policy as a mechanism to ensure that the shareholders receive a return on their invested financial capital.
- The board agreed with using free cash flow as a measure but suggested that the policy should define the term and then explicitly provide for capital expenditures within an established range. (Up until now, management has been free to budget whatever we feel is needed for capital expenditures from year to year; this would be a big change for us.)
- The board suggested using three- or five-year rolling averages to smooth out distributions and increase management's ability to plan.
- The board also suggested that the policy explicitly provide that the board could eliminate the dividend in any year after consulting with the owners. (We debated this for quite a while; the owners at first wanted to be able to override the board, but the board made a good case for needing flexibility to deal with business emergencies and the owners ultimately agreed.)
- The board agrees in concept with creating a war chest but felt that additional work needs to be done to determine when and how it can be tapped. Is it only for acquisitions or investments? Can it be tapped in an emergency? Would it make sense to create a separate division or even a separate company to evaluate opportunities, especially if they are in different businesses than

Owen Products? The board suggested creating a committee of one board member and one representative from the Owners Council to draft the policy for review by both groups.

Christopher has been interested in this discussion with the board as he is at work on the business plan for his company. He has pointed out to us that if we opt to invest in his business, we should not expect a return on capital unless or until the company is sold. No dividends there; but if his plans come to fruition, there should be a substantial payoff within the next decade as well as the creation of enterprise capital that can be leveraged into still other businesses.

CHAPTER

15

Policies

Policies encourage consistency in decision making and promote investment by groups in long-range thinking and planning.

Once the foundational work of creating the forums has been done, once members of the forums develop a working level of consensus and become more comfortable with their roles and responsibilities, and once intergroup efforts begin to bear fruit in the form of more effective communication and collaboration, engagement will increase steadily throughout in the family-business system.

Over time, the forums may wish to articulate policies to guide decision making, particularly around issues that can be expected to arise more than once. A policy sets forth a decision agreed upon by two or more of the forums or provides the parameters within which a decision will be made, thereby providing guidance and helping to manage expectations of the groups vis-a-vis each other. Policies encourage consistency in decision making and promote investment by groups in long-range thinking and planning. They also make inter-forum decision making more efficient and reduce the likelihood that a given topic will crowd out other topics; once the policy is set it can be expected to remain in place unless and until there is a substantial change in circumstances.

Common topics for policies are:

Topics	Participating Forums
Distribution and reinvestment policy	Owners Council and Board of Directors
Share transfer policy	Owners Council and Family Assembly
Family employment and compensation policy	Owners Council, Family Assembly, and Board
Privacy and confidentiality policy	Owners Council, Board of Directors, and Family Assembly
Trust reporting, compliance, and disclosure policy	Owners Council and Family Assembly
Corporate charitable giving policy	Owners Council, Board of Directors, and Family Assembly
Borrowing policy	Owners Council and Board of Directors

Which policies should be addressed first depends on the core capital, shared purpose, and vision of the particular business and family. For example, if the core capital includes extensive intellectual property and knowhow, and the shared purpose includes fostering family employment, the Family Assembly and Board of Directors might jointly adopt a family employment policy setting forth a general policy in favor of hiring family members and then providing certain boundaries to prevent unequal treatment between family and non-family employees:

- The Owners Council seeks to encourage family employment as a means to sustain the human and enterprise capital.
- Management is encouraged to hire a family member if a suitable position exists and the family member is qualified for the role.
- Family members are strongly encouraged to obtain graduate degrees or technical training in subjects relevant to the business. Tuition assistance may be provided by the Education Fund established by the Owners Council.
- The family employee is subject to the same rules and policies as a non-family employee.

- A family employee will be paid the same rate of compensation as a non-family member in the same job having the same qualifications and experience.
- Disciplinary matters regarding a family employee are within the jurisdiction of the human resources department.

Imagine a different family business, one whose core capital includes a highly recognizable brand that bears the family's name. The shared purpose includes nurturing the business to maintain steady growth while harvesting some capital for entrepreneurial activities. To ensure that the value of the brand and the family name is protected, the Owners Council of such a business might work with the Family Assembly and the board to develop a publicity and branding policy that reflects how the brand and name should be used in family, business, and entrepreneurial activities:

- Our brand is one of the most valuable assets within our pool of core capital. It inspires the trust and respect of our customers.
- Our family name is a critical element of our brand, and benefits the extended family financially and socially.
- As a family, we commit to behaving at all times in a manner that will support and benefit our brand. The Family Assembly has developed a code of public conduct to clarify the behavior we as family members expect of ourselves.
- As a business, we commit to ethical and responsible business activity that supports and does not damage our family name. The board and owners have developed a code of business conduct to clarify our expectations regarding ethical conduct by our business and management team. Our brand standards are approved by board and Owners Council in consultation with family.
- Any change in the use of our brand or tagline must be approved by the Owners Council in consultation with the Family Assembly before it is adopted.
- All entrepreneurial activities that intend to leverage our brand core capital must be approved by the Owners Council and conducted in compliance with the code of business conduct and the family's code of public conduct.

A policy reflects an agreement between two or more forums. When a policy is under development, it can be helpful for the participating forums to establish a joint task force to develop a draft of the policy, which will reduce the problems that might be encountered when a large group with potentially diverse interests takes on a wordsmithing project. The draft policy is then reviewed and voted on by each of the forums. A policy should always include the procedures by which it may be amended.

Policies are living agreements. Owners who have seen their ancestors' attitudes toward dividends, reinvestment, or family employment become unquestioned assumptions within the company's culture will recognize the importance of reviewing each policy from time to time to ensure that it continues to serve the purposes for which it was established. Major changes in circumstances—a recession that substantially cuts into the business's margins and profitability, a major change in the regulatory environment, or the acquisition or formation of a new division or business line—all warrant prompt review of existing policies to ensure that they remain appropriate and effective.

PART IV

Three Challenges: Hats, Trusts, and Outside Investors

Introduction to Part IV

An individual who manages the business or plays a prominent role on the board, who serves as trustee of a trust that is an owner, or who is not related to the family but has made a substantial investment in it will have a very different perspective from other family owners.

When a founder passes ownership of a business to children and grandchildren and at least some of the new owners don't work in the business, the issue of ownership decision making comes to the fore. If the owners see themselves as bystanders, enjoying the benefits of ownership and trusting in those who run the business to make good decisions with their capital, then ownership decision making will be relatively unimportant—the owners will be invited to a shareholders meeting once a year, but otherwise their formal contact with the business will be minimal. The new owners may be following widely dispensed advice: "You inherited these shares—don't rock the boat."

But not all owners are willing to take a passive role. Family business owners have more at stake than money. Their ownership stake may represent a substantial part of their net worth, and it also represents investments of human capital and enterprise capital that have been created over many years—their relationships with each other and the wider community, the innovative products, services, and systems that have brought value to the business and its customers, the legacy of their shared past, and the opportunities that all the core capital can generate for the owners and the wider family in the future. The paradigm of engaged ownership offers these owners an opportunity to articulate their shared purpose and vision for the future of their ownership, enables them to provide high-level guidance to the board, and gives them a sharper, clearer voice and role in business decision making.

Yet, even those owners who aspire to engaged ownership may find that their individual perspectives and circumstances stand in the way of their finding a common shared purpose and vision for the future of the business. In particular, an individual who manages the business or plays a prominent role on the board, who serves as trustee of a trust that is an owner, or who is not related to the family but has made a substantial investment in the business will have a very different perspective from other family owners. Engaged owners will need to recognize and accommodate the challenges and demands that such owners may bring.

Owen Family—June 6, 2013

Amanda Owen Cooper

When Dad died and left us his shares, and when the board named Mike president of the company, none of us thought things would change much. After all, Dad owned 75 percent of the shares and ran the company, so Mike's job wouldn't be much different, right? But in some ways it has been harder for Mike than it was for Dad. Martha, Christopher, and I are far more active than Dad's Uncle Fred ever was (and Fred was part of management for most of his life, working for Dad, so he had an incentive to do what Dad wanted). There have been times when Mike has accused us of meddling in decisions that belong to management, and sometimes his accusations were true, especially at the beginning—we were always trying to tell him how to run the company at first. It took us a while to realize that the owners are responsible for the highest level of strategy and really shouldn't deal with management. Our avenue into the business is through the board. Once the board got used to us and our focus on core capital, we began to work together better.

Mike was also worried that our interest in investing in new business opportunities might mean that Owen Products would slowly be starved for capital while we invested in projects that seemed more exciting or potentially profitable. However, being part of our discussions about CombuSynth has made him more enthusiastic, and he has been seeing ways in which Owen Products enterprise capital might help Christopher, and vice versa.

Having an Owners Council has been helpful for Mike in multiple ways. Over the past two years he has learned to look at business questions from different perspectives; sometimes he even stands in one place to answer as president of the company and then physically moves to another place to answer as an owner. The discussion with the board about the dividend policy was particularly difficult for him, because the policy will constrain his choices as president. He has a capital budget and he is expected to generate sufficient free cash flow to enable payment of dividends. However, the policy has built-in flexibility now, thanks to the board's input, and Mike has realized that the multilevel focus on strategy has improved the company's planning overall. What he and his management team have lost in decision-making freedom they have gained in support and focused input from the board and owners. Since we're all aiming for the same target—the owners' vision—the planning process is less contentious. There are still hiccups, and we don't always define the same term the same way, but the process is more transparent and the discussions are more coherent than they used to be.

16

When an Owner Also Runs the Enterprise

> For an owner-manager, the day-to-day challenges of running a business may crowd out thoughts about ownership and core capital.

When an owner also leads the business, her multiple roles may make it more difficult to reach consensus around shared purpose and vision with other owners and the risk of conflict among them may increase. The source of the conflict isn't hard to identify: for an owner who also leads the business, running the company is her occupation and often a preoccupation as well. The drive to achieve business success that is the hallmark of many of the most successful family managing owners can overwhelm their thinking as owners. Running the business is their primary focus, and it can be difficult for them to step back alongside their fellow owners and think about core capital more broadly. Even for those managing owners who want to be mindful of ownership issues and the vision of their fellow owners, the day-to-day challenges of running a business may crowd out thoughts about ownership and core capital.

A founder not only builds a business, he creates a culture and an established pattern of decision making around business issues. A child who succeeds the founder in running the business can find it difficult to make decisions together with other family members who own shares but don't work in the business, because these non-managing owners don't have the same level of information about the business, or even a common vocabulary. Furthermore, joint decision making around ownership issues often simply isn't part of the culture of the business. Particularly if she worked for the founder-parent for a time, the owner-successor may well have adopted the parent's systems and ways of doing things, along with his values and attitudes about conducting business and his decision-making style. The challenge is, assuming the founder controlled all the shares of the business, he never had to deal with the challenges of group ownership, and so his decision-making system, which the successor child has now taken on, doesn't reflect the habits of mutual education, discussion, consultation, and shared evaluation that are necessary to achieve engaged ownership.

For purposes of this chapter, it may be helpful to imagine a successful business owned by three siblings. One sibling, the youngest sister, serves as president; the two brothers have substantial professional careers outside the business. All three inherited their ownership—each owns one-third of the shares—upon the death of the founder, their father. The siblings are close and feel a strong bond with the business and have recently opted to form an Owners Council to govern their ownership of the business.

What are the issues that might create substantive conflict between them?

Shared Purpose and Vision

Talking about core capital together with fellow owners and recognizing the array of core capital both inside and outside the business may help a managing owner to consider the issues through an ownership lens rather than a management lens.

Discussion around the question, "Why do we want to be owners of this business together?" may be more rancorous when the group includes an owner who runs the business and others who don't, especially when the owner in the business (in this case, the president) doesn't own a controlling interest. If the founder exhibited a business-first mentality, the notion that the owners' shared purpose and vision for the core capital should drive business decision making may be foreign, and a managing owner may have more difficulty adapting to such a change in focus.

A managing owner may also feel that she—like the founder before her—should have full control over the business, that the strategic plan for the business should guide business decision making, and that the shared purpose and vision of non-managing owners therefore is less important, or even irrelevant, to business decision making.

To bring a managing owner into conversation with non-managing owners, it can help to begin with a group discussion. A retreat, preferably with a facilitator skilled in working with family businesses, at a conducive offsite location, offers the chance for the owners to delve into issues and not merely skim over the top of them. They will want to avoid holding the retreat at the business office, where proximity may trigger thoughts of management issues rather than broader questions of shared purpose and vision. All the owners answer the question, "Why do we want to be owners of this business together?" and talk openly about their interest in becoming more engaged *as owners*. This exercise may help the managing owner recognize that she is not in it alone, and that the Owners Council offers support, direction, and vision for the future. Talking about core capital together with fellow owners and recognizing the array of core capital both inside and outside the business may also help a managing owner to consider the issues through an ownership lens rather than a management lens.

Conversation around how capital might be deployed can be difficult in some families: there is an innate fear that capital that isn't reinvested in the business will be spent on frivolous purchases or otherwise frittered away. The business thus comes to be seen as a sort of virtuous piggy bank. One of the virtues of having a strong Owners Council is the opportunity to discuss the potential advantages and disadvantages of redeploying capital into new entrepreneurial ventures or ideas. By looking at the potential opportunities of creating new core capital, especially by investing in the talents and interests of young family members, the conversation around core capital can become more invigorating and enlightening.

Allocating Decision-Making Power

Even if she can find consensus with her fellow owners regarding shared purpose and vision, a managing owner may find it more difficult than a non-managing owner to bring an open mind to the process of allocating decision-making power among the Board of Directors, Owners Council, and Family Assembly. An owner-manager who has had formal business education or experience working for a public company may think about corporate governance in terms of the public company model of management- and board-centric decision making. She may find the exercise of reallocating decision-making power to increase the role of owners off-putting and possibly even threatening: because the default decision-making structure set forth in most corporate statutes effectively concentrates decision-making power in the board and management, a reallocation of decision-making rights and powers in favor of the owners becomes a potentially revolutionary exercise.

The thought of giving up any decision-making authority may cause a managing owner to become concerned that she won't have the leeway she needs to run the business, or that the non-managing owners will meddle in day-to-day decision making. She may feel that her fellow owners don't trust her abilities and don't grant her the respect that previously was accorded to the parent. Even the concept of creating a forum for ownership work may be very foreign to a managing owner, whose day-to-day role focuses on business decision making and who may wonder what all the fuss is about.

To help owner-managers practice thinking from the perspective of owners, it can be helpful to undertake a thought experiment. Ask all of the members of the Owners Council to imagine that, thanks to a distant cousin with no heirs, they have just inherited all the shares of a substantial and successful business in an industry they know little about. The business is run by a non-family CEO, and their shares represent the majority of their personal net worth. What would they want to know about the business? What issues would concern them? What controls might they desire? How might they think about their ownership and the opportunities and risks it represents? This thought experiment can help managing owners to reorient around ownership issues and help them to recognize that the desire to reallocate decision making doesn't stem from personal criticism or disrespect on the part of the non-managing owners, but rather from a desire to invest capital wisely and, when appropriate, to redeploy it more optimally. To continue the thought experiment, ask: What is the difference between owning that business and owning our business? How does the legacy of our ownership and management affect our thinking about the business?

Compensation versus Dividends

Conversations about compensation and dividends raise sometimes uncomfortable questions of what is an appropriate return on effort versus on capital.

The issue of how the business determines compensation and dividends can divide owners who work in the business from those who don't. *Compensation* refers to the salary and bonus paid to an employee; *dividend* refers to a distribution made by a corporation to its shareholders in proportion to their percentage shareholdings.

Conversations between managing and non-managing owners around compensation and dividends can become tense because the subject matter suggests a zero-sum game between employees and owners, with managing owners in the middle being pulled from both sides. Such conversations also raise questions of what is an appropriate return on effort versus on capital. Engaged owners will find that developing separate policies around compensation and dividends may bring clarity to the question of how profits and free cash flow generated by the business will be divided among employees and owners. A compensation policy will focus on the procedures by which salary and, particularly, bonuses for a managing owner and other leaders should be calculated; a distribution policy will focus on the procedures by which the dividend should be calculated and paid to all the owners. Spending time educating all owners about compensation and dividends, and then considering what policies will promote the shared purpose and vision, can help to keep concerns and anxiety at a more manageable level.

As it reviews existing policies, a newly constituted Owners Council may find that the founder used compensation, not dividends, as the primary mechanism to pull money out of the business, and that this policy has clouded the group's thinking around compensation and dividends. The strategy of pulling money out of the business via compensation and bonuses is commonplace and makes good business sense: the Internal Revenue Service permits businesses to deduct reasonable compensation in computing income for income tax purposes, but not dividends. So long as every owner also works for the business in some capacity, it can be more cost effective for the business to pay compensation than to declare dividends. That is why we often see small businesses where every adult member of the family has a job—at least on paper.

Over time, though, the compensation structure of a company that uses compensation as the primary means of distributing cash to owners can become distorted. Pay for an owner who works in the business may come to exceed, sometimes wildly, pay for a non-family employee in a similar position. Such wide pay-grade variances can foster a "them-versus-us" attitude among employees, damaging employee morale. Whereas dividends by definition are paid in fixed proportion to shares owned, excess compensation may become untethered from strict proportionality, with employee-owners' paychecks coming to represent an amorphous mix of wages for work done, dividends for shares owned, and additional cash for reasons known only to the controlling owner. If the leaders of the business determine that belt-tightening is necessary and decide to reinvest free cash flow, it can be more difficult to take away compensation than to revise a dividend policy.

Owners who have inherited their shares and don't work in the business will want to be mindful that a business founded and led by managing owners may have developed a culture that favors work and rewards effort rather than capital. After all, the core capital of the business likely was born of hard work, ingenuity, and reinvestment, not outside financial capital. In such a culture, non-managing owners may be seen by those who work in the business as parasites who don't add value and who want to pull out cash that rightfully belongs to the business. This attitude is common, particularly in the United States and other countries where inherited wealth is seen as unearned and therefore undeserved. In such a culture, it can be difficult for non-managing owners to feel comfortable presenting a case for dividends, even though the financial logic is clear: the owners' equity capital supports the ongoing operations of the business and so should earn a return, just as suppliers of labor, goods, and services receive a return.

Redeploying Financial Capital

Does it make more sense to keep investing in the existing business, or to redeploy some of our assets into new or different ventures?

During conversations about shared purpose and vision, engaged owners will want to consider how capital might be redeployed into investments and activities outside the business. Joining into a conversation about pulling capital out of the legacy business may be tremendously difficult for a managing owner, whose career has been spent at the business and whose sense of self-worth and achievement is tied to the performance of the business. A managing owner might ask: Does this conversation mean that my fellow owners don't trust me to manage the business in our mutual best interests? Do they not believe in the strategic plan? Do they not value the legacy that our father created? The conversation can become anxious and highly personal, or even shut down completely.

However difficult they may be, conversations about sustaining core capital are important. Excellent management is no guarantee of long-term business success: customers' needs and tastes evolve, regulations change the economics of an industry, and technological revolutions generate newer and better substitutes. A well-run business will evolve over time by anticipating changes in the market and the environment and adjusting to take advantage of them. Forward-thinking business leaders will see at least some of these changes coming and will build strategic and tactical responses into the business plan.

What senior management may not see are the alternative investment opportunities that arise outside the business but within the family's human capital. Does it make more sense to keep investing in the existing business, or to redeploy some of our assets into new or different ventures? As the members of the rising generation encounter new ideas in school or on the job, they may see ways to combine them with financial capital to create entirely new businesses and enterprise capital. Should the business hire these fledgling entrepreneurs so that their ideas can be nurtured there? Or are those ideas so different that they warrant an investment in a new enterprise? What options does the Owners Council have if a member of the rising generation presents an attractive business plan?

The Owners Council may decide as a group that investing in the human capital represented by the next generation is part of their shared purpose and a good use of their capital. If they use personal assets to invest, or deploy all or part of the existing dividend stream, the new business can be funded without any change in the existing business. But if the capital demands of the new venture are greater than can be funded with personal assets or dividends, the Owners Council may seek to redeploy capital from the legacy business, perhaps through some combination of financing, redemption, or cross-sale.

For the Owners Council, the conversation around funding a new business venture will be a critical test of the strength of their shared purpose and vision. A managing owner may look askance at her fellow owners' idea of funding a new opportunity by pulling operating capital from the business (especially if the Owners Council previously approved the existing strategic plan), and with good reason. Generally, while there may be cash on the balance sheet, it is spoken for—earmarked for operating capital, capital investments, or strategic acquisitions. Pulling cash from the business, whether by limiting capital expansion or acquisition plans, or leveraging the business by borrowing for the purpose of making distributions, will have potentially negative consequences for the long-term performance of the business. The Owners Council would be wise to acknowledge and discuss the tradeoffs involved, in detail, with the goal of coming to consensus around a path forward.

Owen Family—September 2, 2013

Martha Owen Jones

At the Owners Council meeting today, we spent some time discussing the redemption of the shares held by the trust Uncle Fred created for his son, Alfred. It wasn't a small transaction for the company, and it certainly constrained our cash flow. Amanda thanked us again for doing what was right for Alfred and for honoring our shared purpose even at the immediate expense of the company.

Amanda told us an eye-opening story she had heard at a recent family business conference. The business in question was owned 100 percent by a single trust, created for the benefit of the founder's three children. The oldest brother served as president of the business; his younger brother ran the accounting department, and their youngest sister suffered from severe alcoholism and had difficulty keeping a job. The trust company of a major bank served as trustee. About a decade after the father's death, the company received an unsolicited offer from a competitor. The founder had always put the business first and believed that his children should make their own way in the world. He had instilled the same strong value in the oldest son; the son advised the trust officer not to sell. But the dividends from the business were not sufficient to fund the medical expenses of the younger sister, much less the college educations of the middle brother's children, and the trust officer raised the question of how else the trust would meet its obligations to the beneficiaries. Against the wishes of the older son, the trust company sold the business.

This story shocked me a bit, because I was sure that the founder had not intended that the trustee would be able to sell the business against the wishes of the son running the business. It also made me recognize that not all owners and families have the same shared purpose, and that trusts can create issues because they create formal legal obligations to beneficiaries that would not be owed to "ordinary" shareholders. Trustees get caught between their duties to the beneficiaries and their interest in seeing the company become successful, as Amanda was before Owen Products redeemed Alfred's trust. I wondered aloud why anyone would put shares of a family business in trust, and Amanda reminded me that trusts can protect shares and may also make estate planning more tax effective. A knowledgeable lawyer who understands family businesses can help make sure that the trust is drafted to reduce the conflicts that the trustees face. Furthermore, a trust can be designed to give more power to the beneficiaries, or less—basically, a trust can be custom tailored. She reminded us that our mission includes ownership succession planning. We as owners need to begin working on this.

17

When an Owner Is Also a Trustee

A trust divides ownership: the trustee is the legal owner of the shares and holds them for the benefit of the beneficiaries of the trust.

When a trust owns shares in a family business, ownership decision making must accommodate a fiduciary perspective. A trustee of a trust that owns has legal fiduciary duties to the beneficiaries that circumscribe her ownership choices. To operate effectively the structure, membership, goals, and tasks of the Owners Council will need to take into account the purpose of the trust and the roles of the trustee and beneficiaries.

Increasingly, business owners are transferring shares in trust rather than outright, particularly those who reside in jurisdictions that impose gift, estate, inheritance or death taxes on non-sale transfers. A trust can offer tax advantages, creditor protection, and professional oversight for a critical family asset. If an owner feels anxious about whether her children and grandchildren will be capable shareholders, she may be more comfortable putting the shares in trust than gifting them outright. It may ease her concerns about the problems that might arise if shares are sprinkled among descendants over several generations and many individuals come to own non-controlling interests.

In essence, a trust divides ownership: the trustee is the legal owner of the shares and holds them for the benefit of the beneficiaries of the trust. The trust document spells out the rights and responsibilities of the trustee around administration of the trust, investment of trust property, and distributions to beneficiaries. The trustee's decision-making rights and obligations are also dictated by the governing law of the trust. In particular, trust law imposes fiduciary duties of care and loyalty, and a trustee who breaches a fiduciary duty can be held personally liable.

Purpose of the Trust

When the trustee is not an insider—for example, when the trustee is an advisor or corporate trust company—there is a risk that he will not understand either the business or the shared purpose and vision of beneficiaries for the future of the business.

A family might create a trust to hold shares for one or more of the following reasons, and so understanding the purpose of the trust will help determine the membership and goals and tasks of the Owners Council.

- *Minimizing taxes.* An estate planner might recommend a trust as part of an estate and income tax minimization plan. Used in this capacity, the trust is primarily a tax-advantaged conveyance mechanism; the point is to reduce or eliminate a tax levy upon the grantor's death that might otherwise require the company to be sold or stunt its growth opportunities. The family's intent is that their children—the beneficiaries—will still have the levers of corporate control that they would have had had the shares been given to them outright.
- *Protecting shares from divorce or creditor claims.* A lawyer may recommend a trust as an alternative to a prenuptial agreement, in order to avoid the risk of shares passing to a child's divorcing spouse in the event of divorce. Here again, the family's intent is that the beneficiary will still have control, but that share ownership will be protected and kept in the family.
- *Providing a stand-in owner when beneficiaries are incapable of acting.* The family may be concerned that a beneficiary may not be ready to take on the responsibilities of engaged ownership, whether because of youth, illness, financial or legal troubles,

or some other circumstance. The trustee becomes the stand-in decision maker whenever a beneficiary is incapable.

- *Concentrating ownership.* The family may want to avoid the problem of share ownership being divided into smaller and smaller fractions as the family grows. By holding the shares in a single trust (or perhaps in separate trusts for each branch of the family) decision-making power will remain concentrated.
- *Concentrating control while equalizing financial ownership.* The family may want to concentrate ownership control in the hands of one person—perhaps the next leader of the business— while dividing the economic value of the business interests equally among all of the children.

When the trust has been created primarily for tax purposes and the intent is that the beneficiaries will take an active role in ownership decision making, the beneficiaries will reasonably expect to be included in the membership of the Owners Council along with the trustee. The beneficiaries' voices will be critical to developing the shared purpose and the vision for the future of the business and the trustee will be expected to vote and act accordingly.

When the trustee is not an insider—for example, when the trustee is an advisor or corporate trust company—there is a risk that he will not understand either the business or the shared purpose and vision of beneficiaries for the future of the business. The grantor of the trust and the Owners Council will want to take time to educate the trustee about the business and the family, to avoid the risk that the trustee will base decisions on his personal assumptions of what the beneficiaries want or need, rather than the shared purpose and vision. (Furthermore, the trustee may want to undertake a shared purpose and visioning exercise with the grantor, if he is still living and with the beneficiaries as well, to make sure he understands their positions.)

Where the purpose of the trust was to provide for a stand-in for a beneficiary who is unable to act, and the trustee will exercise the ownership decision-making power for a lengthy period, the work of the Owners Council might instead focus on education: first, education of the trustee about the business, core capital, shared purpose, and vision, and then second, education and preparation of beneficiaries so that they can come to assume a greater role in decision making over time.

Where the trust was designed to concentrate control or to separate control from the economics of ownership, the Owners Council will play a different role. In this instance, the trustee is a business insider (and, quite possibly, an owner of shares individually) and so will have a deep understanding of the needs of the business; in many ways, this structure will replicate the control held by the founder. The challenge for the trustee in this case is to balance her business decision making with trust decision making, given the constraints of trust law. From a purely legal perspective, beneficiaries of a trust don't have a right to participate in decision making around the business, unless such rights are explicitly included in the trust agreement, and so in that respect the trustee is free to make decisions. However, from both a practical and a legal perspective, the trustee does not have unfettered ability to act, and may face personal liability if her actions breach the duty of care or loyalty.

The Owners Council can help the trustee manage his responsibilities, promote effective communication with the beneficiaries, and avoid personal liability.

Obligations of the Trustee

> Whereas an individual investor who owns shares of a business is generally free to make ownership decisions as she chooses, a trustee must act not in his own interests, but in the best interests of the beneficiaries of the trust.

The trustee must act in accordance with the terms of the trust and applicable law, all guided by the grantor's intent. Whereas an investor who owns shares of a business is generally free to make ownership decisions as she chooses, a trustee must act not in his own interests, but in the best interests of the beneficiaries of the trust. "Best interest" is measured not from the standpoint of an investor, but from the perspective of an individual. For instance, if the trust requires distributions for the beneficiary's "health, education, maintenance, and support," the trustee may be obligated to vote to increase dividends or redeem shares to generate enough trust income to ensure that the beneficiaries' needs are met, particularly if there are no other financial resources available, even if that decision would run counter to the strategic plan for the business. A trustee who also runs the business may thus find her roles at odds with each other, and may find that serving as trustee significantly constrains her choices as leader of the business.

To fulfill her fiduciary obligations, the trustee will need to understand the needs and interests of the beneficiaries so that she can factor that information into ownership decision making. The Owners Council can be a useful forum for gathering and disseminating information and for building rapport and mutual understanding between the trustee and the beneficiaries.

Beneficiaries Assembly

Where ownership of the business includes individuals as well as trusts, or includes separate trusts for different branches of a large family, it may be useful to create one or more Beneficiaries Assemblies. A Beneficiaries Assembly is tasked with educating the beneficiaries about the trust and providing an ongoing forum for trustee–beneficiary discussion. A trustee becomes privy to substantial amounts of private and confidential information about beneficiaries (for example, about beneficiaries' income level or personal health issues) that will be important for trust decision making but not relevant for business decision making, and so conducting trust-level discussions in a forum separate from the Owners Council can help to manage information flow on sensitive topics. The trustees of all of the trusts will also sit on the Owners Council for the purpose of making ownership decisions, but the trust-level information discussed in the separate Beneficiaries Assemblies will remain private.

Core Capital and Trusts

When all or part of the shares of a family business are held in trust, there is a real risk that the engaged owners' conception of the core capital won't align with the trustee's conception of the trust property. Core capital provides a broader perspective on what is owned: whereas the engaged owners who have enumerated their core capital will see a unique blend of financial, human, and enterprise capital linking them to their shared past and offering them opportunities to build capital in the future, the trustee will see primarily financial assets. This divide between viewpoints can be bridged in substantial part by educating the trustee about the core capital, shared purpose, and vision and by having the trustee participate in the Owners Council. However, both the trustee and the other participants in the Owners Council will need to recognize that the trustee is bound by legal constraints—the trust document, jurisdictional law, common law—that constrain her ability to act. Engaged owners who intend to transfer shares in trust will want to educate their lawyers about their business and their core capital well before the trust is established, and to challenge them to draft the trust in such a way that the trustee has the broadest possible freedom under applicable laws and regulations to act as an engaged owner with and on behalf of the trust beneficiaries.

Owen Family—November 30, 2013

Christopher Owen

As part of the business planning process for CombuSynth, I have been talking with potential investors. The first thing I learned is that few investors are willing to be silent partners, at least at the outset. Most are quite demanding. Everyone I've spoken with has distinct requests: a board seat, tagalong/drag-along rights, preferred shares that convert to common if the company is acquired. Most of these were requests that Amanda explained to me and told me to expect (sometimes it is helpful to have a sister who is a corporate lawyer). From my participation in the Owners Council I've learned that owners of private businesses may have different expectations about strategy, goals, and how performance will be measured. Without that experience, I would have just asked for money and looked for the deepest pockets. Instead, I started by developing a shared purpose and vision with my team. Now, I've begun asking potential investors why they are interested in investing and what they expect to achieve from their investment. Do their interests align with ours? Our focus is on commercializing combustion synthesis to create nanocatalysts for solar panels, but we also expect to create additional research opportunities and enterprise capital that will be useful in other industries. For us, research is an important aspect of the work and might slow down profit generation—my investors need to share that vision.

My siblings are interested in investing. I had some very frank conversations with them about what they are hoping to achieve and what kind of involvement they expect. This is a startup, not a legacy family business. I will own a majority of the voting shares and our decision-making process will be less participative than Owen Products'. This is not because I think what we are doing at Owen Products is wrong; it is because we are creating this business and its enterprise capital from scratch, so to speak, and so we need freedom to take risks, make mistakes, and learn. If they are willing to participate on this basis, I would welcome their involvement.

CHAPTER

18

Bringing in Outside Investors

Bringing in an Outside Owner

Whereas the family owners have a shared interest in the human capital of the business and the wider family and an appreciation of the human and enterprise capital that make up their shared legacy, an outside investor is primarily concerned about a financial investment.

Granting shares to a long-term employee, starting an incentive stock option plan, creating a qualified employee stock option plan (ESOP), bringing in an angel investor or a private equity firm, or undertaking an initial public offering (IPO): these decisions can motivate employees, provide investment capital, or generate cash for the owners. All of them will also bring outsiders into the ownership group and thereby change the ownership dynamic. What impact will outside owners have on the family ownership group, and how should an Owners Council be structured to accommodate the interests of outside owners?

Whereas the family owners have a shared interest in the human capital of the business and the wider family and an appreciation of the human and enterprise capital that make up their shared legacy, an outside investor is primarily concerned about a financial investment. An outside owner will be motivated to make decisions that enhance that investment and will have less concern for non-financial interests. An outside owner will want information about the business and its financial and strategic plans. He may request—or require as a condition of his investment—a seat on the board. He will measure success by return on equity, not by return on core capital. He may challenge management's and board's thinking on strategy and tactics. He will also want to make sure there is a ready market for his shares; an ownership interest that can't be sold is worth nothing, regardless of how much the company is worth on an enterprise basis.

Family owners who are focused on core capital rather than liquidity and return on equity may find it difficult to find common ground with an outside owner; family owners who are less engaged may find that the demands of outside owners disturb the peaceful balance of power that has existed heretofore. Thus, an outside investor can disrupt ownership decision making even as he brings useful capital into the family-business system.

If there is discussion at the management, board, or ownership level about bringing in an outside investor, engaged owners will first want to understand why the proposal is being made:

- To reward non-family managers, in lieu of a bonus, and to align their interests with those of the business?

  Shares may be granted to individual employees, or may be held in a stock plan qualified under ERISA. A plan generally appoints a trustee, who will be the legal owner and will make ownership decisions. ERISA law brings into play many of same fiduciary duties of care and loyalty as a trust.

  When considering awarding shares to an employee, it is worth considering what information that employee might reasonably request or demand about the company and its owners. Particularly for families who prefer to keep personal matters private, granting shares may require disclosing more information about the business, its assets, and activities than the family wishes to share. Phantom stock or a performance-based compensation system may be useful alternative strategies to preserve privacy while aligning employee behavior with the business.

- To bring in outside capital to fund capital expansion or acquisitions?

  Bringing in equity capital to fund expansion can be attractive, especially if the outside investor also brings industry expertise and experience. Equity capital may be less risky than debt financing, especially if the business is already leveraged. But an equity funder rarely will be satisfied being a silent partner; she may require a board seat and demand extensive information on an ongoing basis. An equity investor likely will challenge existing policies, especially those that promote core capital of the family owners beyond the business: corporate charitable giving, family employment, perks, bonuses, dividends.

Engaged owners will want to have an open discussion with the board about the advantages and disadvantages of bringing in outside capital to fund expansion or acquisitions. How will the investor's ownership be structured—will it be in the form of common shares or carry a preference of some sort? What will be the dilutive effect on owners' dividends? Will the access to industry expertise be valuable enough to offset the loss of privacy and the focus away from core capital? Would it be better to structure the investment as a joint venture between the business and the investor, thereby providing a degree of separation between the investor and the existing ownership group? The perspective of the Owners Council will be different from the perspective of the Board of Directors on these topics; because the decision will have a major impact on the composition of the ownership group it will be important for Board of Directors and Owners Council to discuss these matters in depth separately and in a joint meeting well before the plan is fully developed.

- To provide liquidity for an exiting owner?

When an owner seeks to exit, perhaps because she can't find common ground with the other owners or needs to monetize her shares quickly, the descendants may struggle to find a liquidity mechanism that balances the exiting owner's wishes against their individual financial needs and the ongoing financial needs of the business. Whether or not the owner seeking the exit is on good terms with the other owners, her interests diverge significantly from the interests of the owners who will stay on, and it will be important for all the owners to understand the full range of options and consult with the board before any final deal is struck. In particular, the Owners Council will discuss the alternatives of redeeming shares or undertaking a cross-purchase to achieve the exit, and determine whether it is feasible to borrow the needed funds rather than bring in a new equity investor. If bringing in a new equity investor is the route ultimately chosen, the owners and board alike will want to be assured that the terms of the purchase are fair to the remaining owners and don't represent an unreasonable dilution of their interests. The owners will also want to learn about the incoming owner and what influence the incoming owner expects. If the new owner will oppose any efforts by the descendants to become more engaged around shared purpose, vision, and core capital, and if borrowing is not feasible financially, they may want to consider whether their long-term interests would be better served by selling alongside the exiting owner. (This example points out the value of including tagalong rights in a shareholders agreement, to provide protections to minority owners.)

Due Diligence

Who is the investor and what is the investor's stated purpose for making this investment in the business?

Before bringing on an outside investor, the owners will want to ask a number of questions:

- Who is the investor and what is the investor's stated purpose for making this investment in the business? Has he or she made similar investments in other family businesses?
- Who will make decisions on behalf of the new owner? (This question is particularly important when the investor is an entity rather than an individual.)
- What are the proposed terms of the purchase and what rights has the purchaser negotiated (board seat(s), information, preference rights)?
- How was the investor identified? Is this investor known to the owners and/or members of the board? If an investment banking firm has brought forth this opportunity, what are the terms

of the deal between the business and the firm and are there any apparent conflicts of interest?

- Does the investor expect an exit within a certain time period?

Restructuring the Owners Council to Accommodate a Non-family Owner

---

An Owners Council that comes to include an outside investor will have a new dynamic.

Once the ink has dried on the stock purchase agreement, the family owners will want to consider how the Owners Council should be restructured to accommodate the new outside owner. For an Owners Council focused primarily on growing and sustaining the core capital in the business, the Council may want to invite the outside owner to participate, at least some of the time, to build alignment. If, however, the Owners Council has traditionally been more focused on a wider view of core capital, and particularly on developing human capital or deploying core capital in other enterprises, it may make more sense to reconceive the Owners Council as two sub-councils: a family-only forum that will focus on shared purpose and the vision for the future of the family's core capital, and a more business-focused forum made up of all the owners that will deal with the ownership questions and issues around capital structure, ownership succession, and business strategy and performance. Either way, the family owners will want to make an effort to understand the investor's viewpoint and objectives and in turn expose the investor to the family's thinking around shared purpose, vision, and core capital.

However it is restructured, an Owners Council that comes to include an outside investor will have a new dynamic. Family owners who participate with an open mind may find that their understanding of the business and possible options for generating and measuring returns on capital will expand and become more nuanced. They may also find that the outside investor's involvement gives them new perspectives on strongly held beliefs around business strategy and finance.

CHAPTER

Epilogue

Owen Family—October 4, 2014

Ali Owen

The Owen Family Assembly hosted a dinner this evening to celebrate Charlie and Owen Products. I miss Charlie—we all do—but

we continue forward as a family. Such a lovely evening—the Family Assembly held the dinner in the old plant, the same place where Charlie's parents hosted a party to celebrate the company's twentieth anniversary back in 1968. I remember attending that party as Charlie's new fiancée, fresh from the West—it was my first exposure to the company's eastern plant, its first factory. Now, here we are, 66 years after John Owen founded the company. Just as in 1968, there were beautiful floral arrangements at each table showing off Owen Products' terracotta pots. On the tables were electronic tablets showing a series of images from the Owen Products' archives. Something old, but also something new: there were pictures of CombuSynth's new commercial lab and the solar-powered devices that can now be made on a commercial basis thanks to the catalysts they create. Christopher officially launched the company this spring, in part thanks to a $2 million investment by Owen Products. It all comes full circle.

The board attended the dinner. They have developed a much stronger partnership with the owners and management than when Charlie was living—then, the board mostly rubberstamped his requests.

There is a real management team now, too. Martha's husband, Ryan, who now heads operations for the western division, has developed an entirely new level of confidence and by all accounts has done an excellent job. Mike had some trouble getting the eastern division team into place but perseverance paid off and Mike tells me that team seems cohesive and effective as well. Martha is thriving as head of the Owners Council and Amanda brings her sharp legal mind to the board.

And Christopher! Charlie worried all the time about our quiet youngest child. Now here he is building his own business focused on such a high-tech application yet drawing on the experience (the kids would call it enterprise capital) that John Owen and David Smith began building back in 1948.

The thing that struck me most about the evening was how proud Charlie would be of his children's leadership of Owen Products, Ltd. They haven't done things the way he would have done them; he would have looked at them like they were crazy if they had tried to explain it all to him. The whole idea of an Owners Council and thinking about ownership as being about core capital, not just the financial return from the shares. Spending time working to articulate their shared purpose and vision—why it is they want to be involved in this business together—rather than assuming that the business should remain at the center of our lives no matter what, and leaping straight to business strategy or tactics.

Working with the board and encouraging Mike to develop a way of running the company that didn't involve one person sacrificing just about everything for the business. Being brave enough to ask tough questions but making sure they were asking them of the right people at the right time. Developing a strategy and plan to maintain and strengthen Owen Products while also building a war chest for new investments. And sticking to their statement of shared purpose and vision and insisting that the board and management do the same. Building the Family Assembly and creating a place where the entire family can talk about the business, the core capital, and our roles.

Has it been easy for them? No; in particular, the months when they were trying to figure out whether to redeem out Alfred's trust, and whether Christopher would ask to have his shares redeemed as well, were very hard on them. And learning to deal with each other in different capacities—Mike as CEO, Amanda as director, Martha as head of the Owners Council, and Christopher as an entrepreneur seeking funding—this took patience and quite a lot of goodwill on everyone's part.

I think if Charlie had known he was going to die early, he might have seriously considered selling the business. He was worried that Mike didn't have the experience or aptitude to follow in his footsteps. His advisors told him that the children would fight—or spend all the money—and he should prune the tree. And I might have supported that plan, because I was worried, too. The statistics about family business continuity are so grim. But now, with all four kids involved in different ways, I see that we were underestimating them. We were also missing the point: the business, and our financial, human, and enterprise capital, belong to us all together. Together, we stand a better chance of building on what we have. They understand that there is more at stake than money, and their engagement promises to carry us forward together.

APPENDIX A

Sample Decision Grid

	Owners (Individually)	Owners Council	Board of Directors	Management Team	Family Council
Financial Capital					
Selection of auditor					
Annual financial plan					
Borrowing above a set threshold					
Acquisition of business or assets above a set threshold					
Sale of assets above a set threshold					
Sale of business					
Dividend					
5-year strategic plan					
Invest in a new business					
Human Capital					
CEO					
CEO compensation					
Board members					
Close facility or downsize employee base by > X%					
Change operating location					
Corporate charitable giving					
Corporate community activities					
Formation/operationg/funding of family council					
Family employment					

Enterprise Capital
Ownership shared purpose and vision
Change brand/logo/tagline
Move business headquarters
Sell intellectual property
Redeploy enterprise capital into a new venture or
business

A   *Set agenda*
D   *Decide*
C   *Be consulted prior to decision*
I   *Be informed shortly following decision*
     Set policy

191

	Owners (Individually)	Owners Council	Board of Directors	Management Team	Family Council
Financial Capital					
Selection of auditor	D	C	C	A	
Annual financial plan		C	D	A	
Borrowing above a set threshold		C	D	A	
Acquisition of business or assets above a set threshold	D	D	C	A	I
Sale of assets above a set threshold		D	C	A	I
Sale of business	D	C	A,C	A	
Dividend		A,C	D	A	C
5-year strategic plan		C	D	A	I
Invest in a new business	D	A,C		A	I
Human Capital					
CEO		C	D		I
CEO compensation			D		
Board members (slate put forth by nominating committee)		D			
Close facility or downsize employee base by > X%		D	C	A	C
Change operating location		D	C	A	C

Corporate charitable giving	D	I	A	C
Corporate community activities	D	I	A	C
Formation/operationg/funding of family council	C			D
Family employment	C	I	C	A,D
Enterprise Capital				
Ownership shared purpose and vision	D	I	I	I
Change brand/logo/tagline	D	C	A	I
Move business headquarters	D	C	A	C
Sell intellectual property	D	C	A	
Redeploy enterprise capital into a new venture or business (unrelated to existing business)	D	I	I	C

A   *Set agenda*
D   *Decide*
C   *Be consulted prior to decision*
I   *Be informed shortly following decision*
     Set policy

About the Author

Amelia Renkert-Thomas is the joint founding partner of Withers Consulting Group, an international family business consultancy. She works with families and enterprises of all shapes and sizes, from entrepreneurs coping with the consequences of liquidity events to large, multigenerational families with highly sophisticated business and investment structures. She helps families to design tailored governance structures, create more effective board structures, form and govern family offices, set up shareholder councils, and make trusts more functional.

Her understanding of the complexities family businesses face stems not only from her consulting work but also from her own family background. She is the former CEO of Ironrock, Inc., her family's fifth-generation manufacturing business, and the granddaughter of the founder of Fisher Price Toys.

Amelia's consulting work fills a void between family dynamics and management consultancy. Her work reduces and manages the conflicts that can be created by structures of ownership, such as voting and non-voting shares, trusts, partnerships, and foundations, all of which are very familiar to Amelia as a trained lawyer. Her work on ownership has been referred to as "the missing piece of the puzzle" for family businesses.

Because of her mix of personal and professional experience, Amelia is often asked to comment in the press and provide training for families and family business advisors alike.

Index